Running Like China

Running Like China

A MEMOIR

SOPHIE HARDCASTLE

Publisher's note: Hachette would like to thank Nate and Sophie for braving the evening water temperature at Narrabeen to capture such a wonderful cover photo.

Published in Australia and New Zealand in 2015
by Hachette Australia
(an imprint of Hachette Australia Pty Limited)
Level 17, 207 Kent Street, Sydney NSW 2000
www.hachette.com.au

10 9 8 7 6 5 4 3 2 1

National Library of Australia
Cataloguing-in-Publication data:

Hardcastle, Sophie, author.
Running like China/Sophie Hardcastle.

ISBN: 978 0 7336 3426 0 (pbk)

Hardcastle, Sophie.
Manic-depressive illness – Australia – Biography.
Manic-depressive illness in adolescence – Australia – Biography.
Authors – Australia – Biography.

616.8950092

Cover design by Christabella Designs
The cover photograph of Sophie Hardcastle was taken by Nate Smith, natesmithphoto.com
Inside back cover photo of author by Craig Peihopa
Text design by Bookhouse, Sydney
Typeset in 12/16.5 Whitman
Printed and bound in Australia by Griffin Press, Adelaide, an Accredited ISO AS/NZS 14001:2009 Environmental Management System printer

MIX
Paper from
responsible sources
FSC® C009448

The paper this book is printed on is certified against the Forest Stewardship Council® Standards. Griffin Press holds FSC chain of custody certification SGS-COC-005088. FSC promotes environmentally responsible, socially beneficial and economically viable management of the world's forests.

For my mum – my crusader

Contents

Foreword

Mental illness can be confronting and it is easy if you have never been touched by it to judge someone, to point blame or to not understand or be scared and turn away.

But with one in five Australians suffering from mental illness a year, we need to understand.

Every day at least six Australians commit suicide and 30 Australians attempt to take their own lives.

With suicide the leading cause of death for young people aged 15–24, we can't afford to turn away.

Most importantly, we need to listen. We need people like Soph to speak out and to help take away the stigma attached to mental illness. We need to ask our friends, our family, our children – RUOK? And, even more importantly, we need to give them the space to answer truthfully, without fear or judgement

Sophie's memoir, *Running Like China*, is a book of love, a story of hope and, most of all, it's a message for anyone struggling with a mental illness of any kind.

I have surfed with Soph since I was eleven years old, but it was through this book that she reminded me if you hold on, ride through the waves that are trying to pull you down, you can resurface and find yourself again.

Laura Enever
Professional surfer
Former Junior World Champion and Rookie of the Year

Prologue

I became China.

That's how I survived.

I was always a fast runner. I loved the movement. I loved the way the wind beat my face and lifted my hair.

'My friend said I was running like China, that's why everyone calls me China,' I said.

'But that doesn't make sense,' they told me, almost angry that my explanation was not reasonable.

'I know,' I said evenly.

I watched them move awkwardly in their chairs, letting slip an exasperated laugh. 'So you run like a Chinaman?'

'No,' I replied calmly, 'just China.'

'China is not something you can run *like*.'

'I know it doesn't make sense . . . I guess that's why it stuck.'

'Okay.' They sighed, and I sensed their dissatisfaction.

But what they didn't realise, what no one realised, was that China was not a nickname. It was a new face . . . a mask I had adopted. China was a second self that stood bright and alive, casting a shadow over my sick self. In the shadow's darkness, no one could see Sophie's marked skin or the way her hands shook. She was safe.

Beneath the cool veil of China, I had time to heal.

1

Over the Fence

I was one and a half when I moved from a cot to the single bed that would cradle my body until late adolescence. My dad has always boasted of the smooth layers of honey varnish he finely applied to finish the bed.

I'm in hospital right now writing this opening paragraph and text him to verify that he varnished but did not build the bed.

His reply reads, 'Just varnished, but nice job, eh!'

I smile and type, 'Yep, fantastic! I love you.'

When I was ten, the bedhead was freckled with Billabong and Roxy stickers that I'd bought from the local surf shop with pocket money. The corner posts had my favourite Nippers medals hanging from them. I'd Blu-Tacked surfing posters to the ceiling and would lie in bed with sun-kissed bodies riding on turquoise water above.

Air I was going to breathe, ocean I was going to bathe in, wild waves that I was going to conquer.

Dad walked in to tuck me in – a tradition he'd carried out since before I could remember. I would cherish his kiss and respond with, 'Don't forget to come in after dinner and don't forget to look out for robbers,' then fall asleep beneath his soft assurance, 'Okay, I promise.'

My ceiling light hung within a yellow paper lantern, swathing the room in a buttery haze. Dad was not quite fifty yet, but his sight wasn't great and so, on this particular night, it wasn't until he reached the edge of my bed that he said, rather surprised, 'Floss, you're crying.'

I don't know why he calls me Floss, neither does he, but I treasure the way it fuses us together.

'What's wrong? Is it what we just watched?' he soothed, brushing back my hair off my reddened face.

'I just don't *understand*,' I sobbed.

We had just watched an episode of *Sixty Minutes*. The story of two young teenage girls, I think they were thirteen.

A double suicide, two young bodies hanging in a tree.

'How could they have done it? How could they not see how amazing it is to be alive?'

Dad smoothed my hot cheeks with his palm and I remember the way he almost chuckled. 'Well I'm very glad you feel that way.'

'Don't laugh at me,' I whimpered.

'I'm not laughing at you, Floss.' He pulled up my frangipani printed bed sheets. 'I'm happy . . . very happy to hear you say that.'

What father wouldn't be?

What father wouldn't delight in hearing his daughter's rich enthusiasm for life?

I started to calm, my breath steadied and my brilliant red cheeks faded to pastel pink.

'Don't forget,' I said, wiping tears from my eyes, 'to come in after dinner and don't forget to look out for robbers.'

'Okay, I promise.' He swept his cool hand across my forehead, before kissing it, and whispering, 'I love you.'

'I love you too.'

Dad turned out the light and left the room, as I sank into a warm pool of dreams.

Seven years later, I'm standing on the cliff's edge. The sky is burnt orange, as if the distant hills are on fire. The ocean beneath is windswept, with white caps racing across the grey like the flailing white manes of wild brumbies. I try to think of my sister, Georgia. Her face always pulls me back over the wire fence.

Nothing.

I imagine how her body would wilt in my absence.

Nothing.

I imagine how her life will shatter into a million pieces.

Nothing.

I imagine some of those pieces she will never get back.

Nothing.

I look over the edge at the dark waves breaking on jagged rocks below. It's the most terrifying moment in my life. Yet I'm not scared in the slightest.

I am desperate, writhing beneath the impossible hopelessness I feel.

I am *so* desperate to escape.

And suddenly, I understand why and I understand how.

I can see the dark shadows cast prematurely over two girls all those years ago. The girls from that story on TV.

On this night, on the headland, I *understand*.

2

The Stitches in my Skin

For as long as I can remember, I have been entranced by stories.

And for as long as I have been able to speak, I have told them.

Back when my hair was in piggy tails and my uniform was like a potato sack, I stood in front of the class and said my news: 'My mum had a baby girl on the weekend, at 2.49 on Saturday afternoon.'

A classmate stuck up his arm. 'What's her name?'

Everyone was looking at me and I supposed they were probably jealous. 'Zoe.' I smiled. 'She's got dark blue eyes like me and Mum, but her nose looks more like my other sister Georgia's . . .'

When we were walking home from school that afternoon, Mum leant down to me and asked, 'Sophie, do you know why Tara and Scott asked where baby Zoe was when I was waiting for you outside your classroom?'

'I wish you'd called me Zoe,' little Gee muttered, trailing along behind.

Mum laughed. 'Georgia, if you were called Zoe you would wish you were called Ashley.'

The words I'd presented to the class that day – along with the song I'd written for my dad who was off at war, which had brought tears to my eyes as my young hand scribbled verses and a chorus, while he *actually* sat in his office designing yachts – weren't real. I knew they weren't. I wasn't delusional when I told the kids next door the plush toy lizard I was dragging along the road behind me on a dog leash was a real lizard . . . I didn't play pretend. I *invented*.

I loved the fact I could fashion something from nothing. Fishing in the pools of my subconscious for a creature that could not physically exist in the real world. It was magic.

It *is* magic.

Years later, Mum and I reminisced over the childhood stories I'd told, my imagination having given birth to baby Zoe. Mum's laugh was raw and it made her eyes water. 'I'm not pregnant,' she boasted, rubbing her stomach as if she were carrying a child. 'It's a love of great food and beer.'

•

Ultimately this is a story. I wish it was an invention, the pain on the page and the cuts in my skin a fantasy. But these words are true.

The story of Sophie and the story of China hellishly intertwined.

My story.

It is a story of how I sank to the seabed, how I drowned, and how I came to the surface to breathe once more.

For those of you who are drowning, those who have been washed ashore, and those who have had to witness this tragedy in a loved one, I can only hope that my story will share insight, but most of all, that it will inspire life.

3

Pockets of Time

As a child I lay on the horizon, on that fine line between the sapphire sea and the pale blue sky.

When I was eleven years old Mum told me, 'One crowded hour of glorious life is worth an age without a name.'

The quote is from a poem by Thomas Osbert Mordaunt, which Mum had read in Tim Bowden's bestselling biography of the world's greatest combat cameraman and extraordinary Australian, Neil Davis. The quote had resonated with Davis and became the motif for his story. I decided I wanted to read the biography too, so Mum and I went to the local library and scoured the dusty shelves for it. The book's face was as weathered as the man's whose story it held. Thrilled, I turned over pages made semi-transparent by the many hands that had touched them.

I read the foreword where Bowden told of Davis' idea of heaven. The combat cameraman wasn't afraid to die. Instead, he believed that as he closed his eyes for the last time, a beautiful naked woman would approach him with a cold beer. She would kiss him, he would drink beer, and their sex would be unlike anything he had experienced on earth. He wasn't afraid, because he would rest eternally in that blissful moment.

With a philosophy that denied the threat of death, he dared to live within one crowded hour.

Yet, even before I heard that quote I was a child cramming intense joy into tiny pockets of time. I saw the world for all its minute beauties and that provoked in me an intense passion for life.

•

There's a photo of Gee and me squished into a coloured box that hung from the pine tree in our yard when we were little. The swing broke when we were older, and Georgia fell rather abruptly on her arse.

We were at one of those big garden centres that smell of mulch, waiting for Mum to pick out plants for her flowerbed, when Gee and I found a wooden trapeze for sale behind a tree house in the children's play equipment section. Mum said if we still wanted it the next time we came back she'd buy it, and so a few months later, Dad was halfway up the pine, wrapping ropes around branches.

At that stage in my life, my eyes would flutter open each morning to a pale sky; I would walk into the backyard, often still in my pyjamas, and climb up onto the trapeze.

As the pastel pink sky became auburn in the east, I would sit and watch the sun blossom in the distance. In between the bird choruses, there was an indescribable silence.

I also spent a lot of time flying on that trapeze. One beautiful afternoon on Mother's Day one year, my family was enjoying a late lunch at an outside table by the garden when I climbed up onto the trapeze, throwing my weight back and forth until I was swinging from one side of the yard to the other.

Although Mum hated me doing it, she'd seen it before. Nan hadn't and as I fell backwards mid-flight, catching myself with only my knees and flipping upside down, she inhaled half the food that was in her mouth.

I scared them, but what they couldn't understand was how it felt, falling in the moment just before my knees latched around the bar.

I thought that base jumpers, and others who fly so close to death that they can taste it on their tongues, were the ones who experienced the greatest sense of living.

'But what if you don't survive?' Mum asked. 'What if you just die . . . for fun?'

I told her that in that moment, before that person's heart stopped, they would have lived ten lives. They would have experienced something the rest of us couldn't even imagine. They would have lived.

I didn't have a death wish, rather I had an extreme hunger for life.

To fall is a moment of uncertainty. Resigning yourself to chance is liberating. Catching yourself is a triumph.

•

As a child, I also drew pleasure and strength from the natural world. What's more, I understood and could appreciate that I was a tiny, yet significant part of one great organism – planet earth.

There is a mulberry tree at the back of my parents' backyard whose branches became extensions of my limbs as a child. Wrapped around it was a tree house that we were forced to dismantle when I was older because the big tree kept growing and the little house could not.

It was an extraordinary place to play. The tree grew through the centre of the floorboards and up through the middle of the plastic roof. Two of its slender brown arms reached up and across onto the rock wall at the back of the property.

When Dad stands at the rock wall's base, it's three times his height. But as far as rocks go, it's rather beautiful. A sea of lime-coloured vines and pink wild flowers cascade down the rock's face. Its head is covered entirely by thick shrubbery and decorated with pea-green trees.

When we were seven or eight, we worked out that we could walk along one arm of the mulberry tree while holding the other and make it up onto the rock. From then on, summer weekends were spent picking wild poisonous berries from spiky vines and collecting them in jars. We climbed trees further into the bush and pulled up roots from beneath the dry leaf floor because they looked like potatoes. We ground up coloured rocks until they were powder, which we stored in pot plants in the tree house. We would add water until it became an ochre paste, then we'd paint the tree, the tree house, the rock and the fence. Our art would bask in the sunlight until the next storm.

The berries we ate turned our lips and fingertips so purple we looked like we had hypothermia in the warm spring air. Often friends would come over after school and we'd eat more mulberries than the birds that nested in the trees above. Poor Mum would always be left to apologise for our friends' blackened uniforms when their parents picked them up.

Two boys had lived there before us, and they had written their names on the outer wall of the little wooden tree house. Beneath it, we wrote 'and then came Sophie and

Georgia', with a permanent marker from Mum's office. Our handwriting was barely legible but it was ours.

At dusk I would sit on the highest branch in the mulberry tree while violet cooled to indigo and the white moon rose.

The mulberry tree was so important to me. It was sacred, but so were *all* trees. Everywhere we went I would climb them.

Later, in high school, a teacher told us how certain programs to rehabilitate those who have abused, as well as those who have been abused, involved taking people into the woods or forests to surround them with trees.

There is something very humbling about trees.

They are quite remarkable; to stand close to one is to share life. The tree inhales the air I breathe out and I draw in the air it exhales.

.

And then there are the mountains.

The first time I saw mountains was in New Zealand with my family. I was eight and we were looking for a new house because Dad had been offered a job in Auckland. The faint kiss of the sun did not suit Mum's dark skin however, so we came back rather quickly to where the sand burnt the soles of her feet.

That trip was also the first time I saw snow but all that I really remember was being intimidated by the enormity of the earth . . . those mammoth bodies of soil reaching higher than the clouds.

I was both frustrated and fascinated by the raw physicality of the mountains in the same way that I was both frustrated and fascinated by knowledge I didn't yet have the intellect to comprehend.

Standing as an eight-year-old on those slopes, I knew there existed a body far greater than my own self, and I just couldn't get my head around it.

However, the most amazing thing about the mountains for me is the air.

It cuts into your lungs and reminds you why you breathe.

4

The Sea and Me

The sea is a shepherd. It guides, it tests, it challenges, it teaches.

I move among its herd.

I was swimming in the ocean before I was born.

Right up until the day I was delivered into this world, Mum was doing laps in Collaroy rock pool, with me inside her. As waves spilt over the rock wall and washed into the pool, we would swim together. We were two bodies gliding through the salt in sync.

Mum said the ocean was in my blood.

When I was a baby, we lived in an apartment on a street adjacent to the surf. On nights when the full moon turned the sea silver, Mum swore that I screamed louder, as if the moon pulled tides of salt water through my veins.

One morning Mum and my dad took me swimming in the sea before work. It was summer and the waves were gentle, the temperature pleasant.

I was two months old and Mum held me in her arms, standing waist-deep as white foam washed around her hips.

A wave climbed over the horizon, a deep blue wall.

Should she dive under? Or would she try to jump over, with the chance that the wave would take her feet right out from beneath her?

Mum looked to Dad and, in his customary fashion, he laughed. 'I don't know!'

As the wave rose before her, she stared through the sheet of turquoise glass and, in a split-second decision, held me close to her chest and dived beneath.

I cannot remember that moment; the first time I swam through the belly of a wave. But my body can remember the sensation. My tongue remembers the taste.

Mum got caught in the turbulence beneath the foam and lost her footing, so she thrust my little body up through the water's skin and into the light of day. Dad dived across to take me from her hands and wrapped me in his arms. Mum surfaced, and it was only as she was wiping her hair from her eyes that she realised I hadn't screamed.

To her utter surprise, Dad and I were dripping wet and *laughing*.

In that moment, Mum says she knew I was going to live a life among the waves.

·

When I was four, I so badly wanted to join Nippers – the program for junior members of surf lifesaving clubs – that, although I was underage, Dad took me round to the local clubs to try and enrol anyway. Long Reef, the beach in between Collaroy and Dee Why, was the only club that would take me. At that point Longy had a mere thirty-two kids across nine age groups and so my early arrival was warmly met.

I was fast at running for my age and gender, and when Mum became my age group manager we fought bitterly over the handicaps she gave me. I remember one day in particular lining up for a 'wade' race where you run into the shallow water, leap over the waves on the shoreline and around a few parent volunteers with water up to their knees, and back to the sand. The other girls were on the wet sand and I was standing on the sand dunes next to the lifeguard tower, fifty-five steps back.

When the race was over, Mum said, 'See, you didn't need to have a tantrum, you still won.'

I gave her a look so foul she probably should have smacked me. The next week I was so far over the sand dune that I didn't hear the start of the race.

The following year Dad became my age group manager and there were far fewer domestic disputes. The girls thought Dad was so cute. He's not plump like a teddy bear, but he is certainly as soft. He thought it was fantastic that they laughed at his jokes. I know he really enjoyed it, and at the end of each year he'd make us all his own little certificates, separate to the normal prize giving, with our nicknames on them. He laminated each piece of paper, rewarding us for some kind of personal feat that was quirky and humorous.

When I was in Under 9s, we went from doing the wade to competing in a board and a swimming race. For several of the girls in our group this was incredibly daunting, but I was thrilled.

My young arms grew strong from paddling as I thrust my little board and tiny body through clouds of foam twice my size.

Long Reef was still a small club back then and I won their first ever branch medal at an inter-club event. I wore a smile that stretched from ear to ear and the medal under my t-shirts for weeks.

As each Nipper season passed, I kept all my branch and state medals on the right bedpost of my wooden single bed. There were so many that they clattered together when I rolled over at night.

I spent hours after Nippers every Sunday on the pink and yellow foam boards. They had plastic hose handles that I gripped as I flew to shore on my stomach. Despite a neck of gold medals, however, I grew tired of riding on my belly. I wanted to rise.

One day, I was paddling my foam Nipper board out the back across the turquoise drink. Dad was swimming several metres away from me, floating on his back, letting the golden orb of summer warm his belly. On the beach the sun was bleaching the sand where Mum sat with Gee on her lap.

I began to paddle as a small wave rose from the sea, it picked me up, and I began to fly.

I don't know quite how I did it, but I remember looking down and realising my feet were on the board.

The water was so clear I could see the sand shifting on the seabed. The sight and sound and feel of the water moving beneath me as I flew towards the shore were the most remarkable things my nine-year-old self had ever experienced.

I rode the wave until my board hit the wet sand and I jumped off, racing across the hot powder to where Mum and Gee were sitting. I was bouncing up and down, waving my arms about while Mum listened to me telling her what had just happened over and over again.

I'd felt as if the air had been sucked right out of my lungs and, in its place, my chest expanded with a new breath that was particularly dry and salty.

The ecstasy of that first wave coloured my cheeks and warmed my skin. It made me dance on the sand. It changed me in a way I will never understand. It was a feeling I will never shake.

By the time I was thirteen I was surfing before and after school. Most nights I was out until the streetlights had come on across the promenade, and even then I wanted to stay out longer.

I was thirsty for the sea.

.

The point break near where we lived is notorious for the ladder in the thick wall of water that breaks behind the rock pool. As the wave climbs onto the rock shelf, it jacks up in sections and creates steps. Even experienced surfers can be thrown into the frothy soup behind the rocks when a step rises in the wave's face unexpectedly. The wave is dark and for a long time it scared the hell out of me. It wasn't until we moved into an orange-brick flat up on the headland that I saw the wave for its brilliance. The wave is dark because it is alive.

I was a thirteen-year-old girl and that wave challenged me. I dropped down its green face for the first time on a bright Tuesday morning before school, riding behind the rocks before it spat me out into the open channel. The ocean was quiet that day and, although the wave was small, a cool blend of fear and elation had my hands shaking as I flew off its shoulder victorious.

As the nights grew longer, and the wave grew colder, I surfed its stomach and flew over its shoulder. Slowly I began to understand it.

That is one of the things I love the most about the ocean . . . every single wave has its own identity. Its shape, its colour, its speed make it as individual as a fingerprint and, yet, in a way, with patience, you begin to understand the character of the break itself. A beachy, a lasting sandbar, a rocky point, a reef; they all have their own distinct traits. Dropping down their faces or getting caught inside their gargling bellies, you get to know them.

You form an alliance. The alliance is intimate, and yet it can kill you.

There are storms that only come two or three times a year. Big storms where the ground shakes as a grey sea thrashes against the shore. The sky turns a deep indigo.

There was one of these storms in autumn 2008 and as the wind began to scream, a cold, salty mist lingered in the kitchen. The southerly wind roared for two nights and two days.

On the third day, we woke to a veil of silence draped over the coast. The sound of absence was almost as remarkable as the screaming wind.

I got out of bed that morning, pulled a woollen jumper over my pyjamas, slid into my Ugg boots, crept down the flight of stairs, out of the apartment block and into the bitter air. The streetlights were still on as I traipsed up to the headland.

The sky was pale purple with a light wash of grey. The smooth sea was stained with black ink, and as I approached the edge of the wet, grass hill, I was electrified by the energy of the ocean. There were already three guys out off the point, even though the moon lingered, waiting for the sun.

Giant mountains of water rolled in, jacking up as they hit shallow water then crashing down onto the rock shelf. I turned around, walked back to the apartment, crept into the room I was sharing with my sister, and put on my wetsuit.

One of my friends met me on the beach that morning. With our boards under our arms, the icy sand made the soles of our feet burn and our bones ache.

As we ran down to the wet sand, the mixture of the crisp cold air, nervous energy and wild excitement had our teeth chattering. Reaching the shoreline, we leapt with our boards before us and landed with our bellies on their waxed decks. We duck-dived the first wash of foam and when we surfaced on the other side our brains were snap frozen.

Together we raced out to the rocky point, telling jokes and stories between duck dives, making the paddle harder as the laughter drained air from our lungs. Yet it also made the paddle lighter as our cheerfulness distracted us from the pain in our arms and winter breathing down our necks.

When we reached the line-up, the men didn't look at us in astonishment as if we were brave, they looked at us in fear as if we were stupid and were going to drown.

If my friend and I hadn't been so keen to outdo each other, we might have been discouraged by their grimaces.

The wave's dark face was three times our height. For a while, the men cut inside us, stealing every wave from behind the rocks. I don't know whether they thought they were protecting us – *if they can't catch any waves, they aren't going to eat it when they fall off* – or if they thought we simply didn't deserve the chance. But we were competitive. We both wanted the first wave, the upper hand, and in fighting each other, we fended off the men. I'm not sure who made it over the lip first, but after we'd both caught a few waves, the guys out there were calling us in. They were impressed.

It was wild; it was ecstasy. It was a magnificent blend of terror and joy that left us barely able to speak.

We had both had several rides when a wall climbed up from the ocean's floor and grew so great it blocked out the black horizon.

'Go!' one of the older men called. I remember his face clearly; he had a white beard and the hair on his head was scarce. His face was brown leather and with a fire burning in his eyes he cheered even louder, 'Go!'

My eyes darted around the water, I was on the inside; the wave was mine.

As my feet landed on the deck of my board and my hands lifted from the rails, the wave jacked up beneath me. In the few seconds that ensued, as the wave transformed beneath me, my eyes met my friend's and I watched her mouth slant downwards.

It was as if I was going into battle. I was about to visit a dark place, I was about to face the enemy, and she looked at me hoping I had enough ammo to fight my way back to the surface.

I gulped in a lungful of air and, as I free fell, time seemed to pass slowly.

Hitting the water, however, was like falling through a sheet of ice. The dark water slapped me red in the face and punched me so hard in the stomach it winded me. Like a rag doll, I was tossed until I didn't know which way was up.

I hit the bottom twice, tearing a hole in the elbow of my wetsuit.

Experienced surfers tell you not to panic, not to fight it. They tell you to relax; it saves energy and it gives you time. In the turbulent, white belly of a wave, *time* is everything.

I did well to remain calm . . . until I heard the roar of another wave breaking on the surface. I was *still* under and the turbulence tossed me violently all over again.

When I finally reached the surface, I pulled my board towards me with my leg rope and tried to climb on. My arms were jelly and for a while all I could manage was getting my torso on the deck, while I heaved clean autumn air into my lungs.

The greatest memory I have of that morning was being washed almost to shore, lying half on my board. The shock had reduced me to tears and, as the light of day broke through the clouds above, I could see, around my head, the stars of night.

It was a harsh reminder that the ocean is alive, and you can no more hold its waves than you can hold the flames of a fire. If you believe you can control it, it will ruin you. Instead, it is humbling to know you are at the mercy of the land and the sea.

I went to school that morning, and sat in my normal seat next to the classmates I always sat beside.

None of them would know how, on that very morning, I had felt the wrath of the ocean as it spun me beneath the breaking waves. None of them would know how drastically different I was compared to the girl they'd sat beside the day before.

With my hair still damp, my nose burning and my pink eyes stinging, I realised I was alive in every sense of the word.

In the wake of that day, I possessed a profound and unswerving respect for the ocean.

Fear of and admiration for the sea became the red and indigo blood that moves through my veins like the summer and winter currents that move through the deep.

5

Chasing the Horizon

For as long as I have had air in my lungs, a competitive streak has stained my skin. Mum has always held that my biggest rival has been myself, and the battles I walked away from victoriously were those where I had fought as an individual.

I didn't like relying on anyone else. If I made it, *I* wanted to make it. If I fucked up, I knew I only had myself to blame.

When I ran on a cross-country track, my face would redden and my chest would ache but the most gruelling race was inside my head. There were many girls who could have run just as fast if not faster than me, but my mind was what won me the race.

At Nipper carnivals, I possessed natural talent, but I also understood the power of the sea and resigned myself to the waves and the vast ocean. I resigned myself to the things I could not control, and harnessed the things I could – my body and my mind. I could never choose the way in which the waves broke; I had no authority to demand a smooth path through the break out to the race cans. I didn't compete with the ocean, only myself.

When I was held back behind a set, the only thing I could choose was how I responded. My mind would will my arms to paddle harder and my legs to kick faster. When my body felt at its limit, my mind would see *more*. Subsequently my limbs would stretch further.

Competitive surfing events though were where I really invested myself. I had sponsors from the age of twelve and, for several years, I thought I was going to turn pro. I remember Mum telling me that it wasn't *all* about the competitions. She told me about the ugly side of the tour and the struggle to make a living for the girls who weren't in the top few. She also told me that there were many people who loved surfing, but went about their work, and surfed morning and afternoon. I told her I didn't care for that simplicity; I wanted a life on the move between competitions; I wanted to cross seas.

I was very lucky to be a part of those junior comps.

At school, I was a little awkward and never truly a part of any one group, but it didn't matter, because I travelled further most weekends than any of them dreamed.

My best friends became those who lived miles away. They invited me into their homes, I ate dinners with their families, I listened to the slight discrepancies in their accents, I surfed their home breaks, I swam in their waters and I lay on their sand.

My travels as a young surfer showed me Australia's eastern shores, which stemmed a deep desire to see *more*.

If I could ride every wave that breaks across this blue planet, it would not be enough, because if I did it all again, *every* wave would be different from the first time. If I visited every city, walked across every desert, trudged through every forest, climbed every mountain, met every person and tasted every meal, it would not be enough because the sun would dawn on a new day and everything would have changed.

Recognising that I can never experience it all, never know it all and never understand it all saddens me, and yet it is the very reason I explore.

The travel also meant I spent long hours beside my greatest supporter: my mum. With seatbelts on, she shifted gears and we drove through days and nights.

She was the one who slept on the bottom bunk in the motels we'd inhabit for the duration of the comps. She was the one who waited for hours for my heat, hours on lay days when the surf wasn't suitable for the event, hours after my heat for the results, and hours waiting for the presentation.

By the time I turned sixteen, however, fatigue was creeping across my body like grey clouds creeping across the sky in the hours before a storm. As my muscles and my mind became weak, so did my fight. I stopped surfing for myself and rode every wave as if it were being scored. Even when paddling out at my home break I'd be kicking myself for every mistake I made. I cared less for the sea, and found myself overly critical of my every move. *That turn could have been sharper, my foot should have been further back, I should have picked the wave behind, my jump-up was too slow.*

Frustration overrode the very joys that had first brought me to my feet.

These impossible standards, coupled with my fading energy, saw me getting knocked out earlier and earlier in each contest until one day I didn't even bother to turn up.

In the end, I began writing about surfing each night more than I was surfing each day.

•

The greatest thing my time surfing the Australian grom comps gave me were those hours beside Mum.

Some drives were as long as twelve hours and, despite the cramps in my bum on the passenger seat, and the pins and needles in my legs, I would relish those hours because they were the ones in which we *spoke*.

Sometimes I feel like Mum and I can speak together in a dialect only we understand, and as the tyres wore on the country roads, we lost ourselves in conversation.

We would often debate, and although Mum's morals and opinions align very closely with mine, she would still find a way to challenge me. But mostly, she would tell me stories and I would sit there in silence, enthralled, as she painted characters and scenes with her words. Hearing about the seas she had crossed and the exotic shores she'd set foot on with my dad when they were professional sailors, I knew I would never live a life in one place.

Many of the characters in her stories became my friends and although I had never met them, they each had a remarkable thing to say.

When we stopped for tea and biscuits at country town cafés, Mum told me about the many flavours of the world and I became hungry for more than the food we were eating.

Most importantly, I learnt that she had had her heart broken, she had been disappointed, her dreams had been shattered, she had been terribly mistreated, but that she had also been drunk on Mount Gay Rum with true friends in the Caribbean, she had laughed until she cried, she loved and was loved by my dad, and she was proud of both my sister and me.

I'd been crushed to learn that she had known heartache and that at times life had beaten her black and blue, and yet I was inspired that she had lived within many crowded hours.

Quite possibly the most significant conversation we had in the car was while driving back from Lennox Head to Sydney. The road was winding through a forest of tall gums and Mum and I were talking about what I was going to become. I told her I was going to travel the world, and I'd write a book, publish it, and then buy a ticket with the profits to the next place, where I would write another book and so on . . . I wasn't going to go to university. I wasn't going to conform to a set social standard of getting a good HSC result so that I could go to a good university so that I could get a good job and work to get a good house with nice things, have a family and then continue working so that I could have a good retirement where I could *then* travel the world.

How many people climb mountains in Peru or stay in backpackers' hostels on the streets of Vietnam or trek through tropical jungles at the age of seventy-five?

Mum seemed somewhat distressed by my plans as I pointed out it's far more common for retirees to wine and dine in city restaurants, go on cruise ships and stay on vineyards in comfortable inns, none of which I was interested in.

Then, with sunlight filtering through a canopy of eucalyptus leaves, Mum turned to me and said, 'I believe that those who are intelligent have an obligation to do something with it.'

She told me I was given my mind for a reason.

'You can't just let it go to waste; if you're smart enough to be a doctor, then you owe it to the universe to use that gift for the benefit of others.'

I guess that I had known deep down what my purpose was for a while; this car trip was simply the first time it had ever been articulated out loud.

Looking across at her I said, 'I don't want to offend doctors because their work is selfless and hard; they are amazing. But I just don't think it would be *enough*. I could only save one life at a time. I could only change one patient's story at a time. Through my writing, I could change the way people *see* the world.'

.

In year 10 – when I was still at the Catholic all-girls school that my nan and her sisters had attended in the 1940s – we had interviews in the late spring with a careers advisor to discuss our futures. I felt oddly superstitious, as if I were meeting a fortune teller. I was afraid she was going to read a path in the lines of my palms that I didn't want to walk down.

The meeting was held in the senior art room. When called in, I sat opposite the advisor at a large bench covered entirely by a crust of paint pigments. The advisor's ears shone pink as the afternoon sun melted in the west and light poured through the window behind her. I smiled and told her that I wouldn't be going to university. Rather bluntly I told her how I was going to travel the world, writing stories that would inspire people.

I had a brown leather folder that held the handwritten words of my first novel on my lap and opened it for her as if to present evidence for my case.

I thought she was going to tell me off. I thought she was going to verbalise the words on every adult's tongue – *completely unrealistic.*

A sheet of silence hung between us as she wrote a very short sentence in her notebook, before she looked up and set her dark eyes against mine. 'Okay,' she said.

Okay? Was she being sarcastic?

'That's what I'm going to do,' I said adamantly

'Okay . . . I believe you. You just walked in here, sat down, and said *exactly* what you're going to do. Every girl who has come in here today has said, I *want.*' She laughed. 'You just said I *am.*'

I smiled, and the meeting concluded.

6

Darkness

Most of the time, we don't notice the darkness . . . Not until we're in the thick of it.

Sure. We see the sun slide behind pink clouds before it disappears below the horizon, but the sky doesn't immediately turn black; dusk lingers with pastel blue and purple chalks.

We don't notice the darkness creeping across the sky . . . Not until the streetlights come on and we look around, and say, 'Fuck, it just got dark quick.'

•

It started when I grew tired.

As a child who ran circles around everyone and everything, the fatigue frustrated the hell out of me.

At fourteen, I would ride my bike for twenty minutes (fifteen if I was powering), my surfboard under my arm and my wetsuit and towel in a backpack, down to the beach after school almost every day. I would surf for an hour and a half, or two, before showering off, getting back on my bike with a heavy wet towel and wetsuit in my bag and riding home for dinner.

Nearing sixteen, I was surfing maybe twice a week, and only when I got a lift to the beach. If I surfed for half an hour before my arms started to ache, it was more than a decent effort.

Mum told me that she'd been tired as a teenager too. She'd napped most afternoons and slept ten-hour nights. She assured me that it was normal; I was just going through the biological changes that would make me an adult. But by the time I turned sixteen I was sleeping fourteen-hour nights.

In the year that followed those nights grew longer.

At school, I soon found that on Monday mornings my eyelids were pink and puffy, my mind was foggy and my limbs were drained. For a while I assumed that it was simply the consequence of being a teenager on a Monday morning, recovering from late nights and booze.

As time went on, however, I grew frustrated, wondering why my friends, who partied harder and later than I did, managed each Sunday to get up earlier than me. How did they wake up with the energy to stride confidently down to the shops for bacon and egg rolls, before parading across the beach beneath a shower of sunlight?

I wanted to know *why* I felt so tired, but I was reluctant to ask anyone because I didn't think the fatigue was a real problem. I didn't think it was something to be taken seriously.

I feared that if I knocked on the school counsellor's door, he would see right through my exhaustion. 'Tired? So what, you just like to party, only people with real problems are allowed in here.'

·

My energy levels diminished for several months before the next thing began to fade: enjoyment.

My friends became less funny. Parties became less wild, boys who I had previously lusted after became less enticing. I stopped laughing, I left birthday dinners early, I shared fewer secrets and I found myself disliking almost every movie I saw or every song I listened to.

Out in the surf, I stopped loving the way I could walk on water. I stopped loving the way my board moved beneath my feet or the way I sat at dusk in the line-up immersed in the indigo sea. I started to resent it. One morning I walked into the kitchen in my school uniform, my hair still wet after a surf, when Mum asked, 'How was it?'

I was pouring milk onto my cereal and looked up at her from beneath a heavy brow. 'Shit.'

At that point Dad chimed in. 'Is it ever *not* shit anymore?'

I don't really know why I kept surfing during those months. I hated it most of the time, and I certainly didn't chase the waves with the same vigour that I had when I was younger. Maybe I held on because I was scared. I was starting to sink and knew deep down that if I lost my place in the ocean, I would lose myself altogether.

•

The acidic combination of fatigue and displeasure gurgling in my belly depleted my motivation. I couldn't be bothered. But a lot of teenagers can't be bothered. Aren't a lot of teenagers tired? Aren't a lot of teenagers grumpy?

Even in hindsight it is incredibly difficult to discern when my standard teenage rebellion became seriously sour.

I mean, off milk is just milk past its use-by date . . . until it starts to curdle.

People only had to compare me to the person I *used* to be to know that something was wrong. The problem was that I was at a new school so no-one knew my normal.

Up until then I had been at the Catholic girls school, but I wanted to be challenged, I needed something to scare me, and so I had moved to a selective academic school. Initially I thrived; I loved the intellectual banter at recess. I loved that conversations had depth. Most of all, I loved the competition. In one year, I climbed from being ranked thirty-second in Advanced English, to equal first in Extension Two English. I was chasing the horizon. However, as the darkness descended, everyone at school just assumed I was a moody character, because there was no reference point to who I had been before.

I was a high girl who threw herself at much older boys and said things she probably shouldn't have and disrupted the class . . . A low girl who moved slowly, and cried at random and said things that sounded kind of off but that seemed okay because that's just how she'd 'always been'.

I saw little of my old friends at the time and was out all weekend every weekend, which worried my mum. I thought I was my own person, a cunning, capable teenager who didn't need *anyone* to tell me what to do.

But isn't that the attitude of most arrogant sixteen-year-olds?

When was the precise moment day became night?

Residue of my former self lingered like the pastel blue and purple chalks of dusk.

I guess it wasn't until I was standing on the edge of the cliff that the streetlights turned on and everyone looked around and said, 'Fuck, it just got dark quick.'

•

One day in October 2010, as I moved into year 12, I stopped the school counsellor in the playground. The sky was white and the air was neither hot nor cold. I told my friends I'd meet them in class and I remember the way they'd hovered awkwardly as if to question, 'Soph, what are *you* doing with *him*?'

Moments later the bell rang and they disappeared into the brick building.

The counsellor said my name and my head tilted slightly . . . we had never met.

'Sorry, I used to work at your primary school,' he said. 'That's how I know your name.'

'Oh.' I laughed sheepishly. 'I thought I recognised you.'

His smile was sweet, but his words were prompt. 'What can I do for you, Soph?'

'I don't really know.'

'When's your next free period?'

I fished out my timetable from my bag.

'Perfect.' He landed a finger on a free time slot. 'Does that suit?'

I tripped over my tongue, 'Yes, yep, okay.'

With a few smooth words and the point of a finger he showed me where his room was, and I nodded as if I hadn't walked past it every day for the last three weeks.

'See you then.'

A few days later, I sat on a soft green couch with my back to the window. There were some mental health pamphlets and information thumbtacked to a corkboard.

The counsellor had two school photos of his daughters in white wooden frames beside his computer. He also had a few drawings the younger one had done Blu-Tacked to the pale blue wall.

I don't remember the finer details of that room, and I think that is because of him. He was honest, compassionate, intelligent and adventurous.

Above all, he wore his heart on the cotton sleeve of his collared shirt.

He was *good*, and for a long time he was my best friend.

I liked him from the start, but it wasn't until our fourth or fifth session that I respected him.

I was on the green couch with my legs crossed and my back slouched when I asked him, 'Are you a psychologist or a counsellor?'

He was a psychologist and I asked what the difference was.

'Nothing really, just a higher level of education . . . a psychologist is more qualified theoretically.'

'Then why do you work as a school counsellor?'

He laughed. 'Friends of mine ask me that all the time. I could make loads more money as a private psychologist with my own practice but I don't believe your quality of treatment should be based on the coin in your pocket. There are kids here whose parents would never be able to send them to a private psychologist . . . That's why I'm here.'

I saw him weekly for a month or so, knocking on his mauve-painted door during free periods.

'Does it annoy you that I'm here?' I asked him once.

'What do you mean?' He swung back in his chair.

'Do you think I'm wasting your time, like *there's nothing wrong with this girl so why is she even here.*'

He sat up straight in his chair, adjusted his collar and as his green gaze held mine, he said, 'You are here . . . *That* is a reason.'

•

When my energy, motivation and sense of enjoyment were extracted, they left a hole. A huge gaping hole. I lost weight. My eyelids puffed with fatigue and my cheeks were hollow, even though my appetite had me eating five full meals a day.

In the month before I turned seventeen, that hole was filled with the most intense sadness I had experienced in my entire life. It was November and I cried hysterically on both my mum's and my sister's birthdays for no apparent reason.

That was the month the sun dipped beneath the horizon.

I began to feel intensely dark waves surge over me at random, and it was as if I would begin to choke beneath the freezing cold water. I would feel complete and utter devastation as if my family was dead, and yet there was nothing to warrant such sadness. Then I would halluci-nate that my skin was tightening around my bones, suffocating me.

The first time it happened, I'd been feeling low for several days when an icy wash of sadness annihilated me.

It was a Tuesday morning and yellow light was streaming in through our windows from the east. Dad found me pacing in the bathroom with beetroot cheeks and my school uniform wet with tears, pulling at my hair as I screamed hysterically.

He asked me what was wrong. Deeply concerned.

When I couldn't answer he asked me again. Louder.

'What's going on?' Mum yelled from downstairs.

Dad asked me *again*, this time angry.

I remember crying and smashing my head against the white tiles before Dad lunged forward and grabbed me.

He took me downstairs and I sat there, pulling at my skin, as my parents asked me over and over what was wrong.

When I coughed up no more than 'Nothing!', Mum waved her hand, turned back to the kitchen bench and said, over her shoulder, 'I don't know why you don't tell us things anymore; you used to tell me everything.'

I didn't know why my skin felt like a straitjacket. I couldn't understand it. There was *nothing* wrong . . .

I couldn't explain it to Mum because I couldn't even explain it to myself.

Mum assumed it was some teenage drama, and wanted me to share the name of the girlfriend I'd had a fight with or the boy I was freaking out over, but with growing concern she took me to our family GP. The doctor had barely opened the conversation when he said, 'These should be the best years of your life.'

I melted into the black leather chair. I knew he was right, but the way he said it was heartbreaking.

We spoke for a few minutes before he said it sounded like I had depression. I told him I was seeing my school counsellor, which pleased him. He then asked, 'Are you suicidal?'

I shook my head. 'I don't think so . . . No.'

'Well I'm going to leave it at that then, you should keep seeing the counsellor at school . . . I'd like you to come back if you start feeling suicidal.'

I told the counsellor in the pale blue room when I was sitting back on his couch.

'Come back when you're suicidal? Is he serious?' He laughed, and I almost did too.

'I'm going to find you a new GP.'

I exhaled with relief.

'I mean . . . that's absolutely absurd.' While his laugh humanised him, it also showed me that no one doctor has all the answers. And as the weeks went on, he taught me that patients have the right to change counsellors or psychologists or psychiatrists until they find one that they gel with. He showed me the value of confiding in someone you trust. Above all, he showed me there is *always* someone there; you just have to be brave enough to knock on the mauve-painted door.

•

The second time my skin tightened was after school a few weeks later. My sister went to a private school where the classes ended later, so I was home first. I was home alone.

I had felt so low that week that I had barely written two words in my exercise book in class that Thursday afternoon. I walked through our front door, up the stairs and got into my bed with my uniform and shoes on. It was there that the sadness swept through every window and pinned me to the bed. I burst into tears and, as my skin began to shrink again, I ripped off my uniform, shoes and socks.

My stomach burned and I stumbled naked into the bathroom, feeling as if I was going to vomit. When nothing came up, I stuck my fingers down my throat and emptied. Acid made my teeth gritty and my tongue sour but my skin had loosened.

After a few weeks, having alleviated these 'episodes' with my fingers down my throat several times by then, I told my school counsellor. I wouldn't have said anything, as I was scared he would convince me to discontinue my one means of relief, except that my sister had caught me vomiting several times. The first time she caught me I denied it and made up a pathetic lie that she could see right through. The second time she caught me it suddenly became a real thing between us. I admitted that I had made myself vomit, but then I made her promise she would not tell *anyone*, not even our parents. I told her that what I was doing made me feel better, but that no one was allowed to know.

My sister silently carried a load that became heavier with every foul secret I dumped on her in the coming months.

When she caught me vomiting for the third time she begged me to stop . . . and so I'd decided to talk to the counsellor about it.

I told the counsellor that it was like I was purging those feelings . . . cleansing myself.

'You know this is incredibly bad for your body, especially your mouth, teeth, throat and oesophagus . . . It's unnatural.'

'Then why is it helping me?'

•

My erratic behaviour and subsequent lows were washed out in the New Year. For January, and the better part of February, my family and I escaped with the belief that what I had experienced was just teenage attitude, stress and drama . . . that I'd just gone through a rough little 'phase'.

I guess that's why it was such a shock when I was hit with another onslaught.

It was a Friday when a lady in red lipstick became more than just my teacher.

I remember that the sky was pale when I truly learnt that the mind could devastate the body without reason.

English was my last class that day and I was sitting at the back of the classroom, with tepid tears pooling on my lower lashes. I didn't touch a pen, or read a word of the material. I just sat there, desperately trying to keep it together.

Halfway through the lesson a dark wave broke through the windows and washed over me, and a river of hot tears flowed.

I remember the confusion mostly. I was *so* sad and *so* hopeless . . . as if I was grieving a tragedy that hadn't occurred. I simply could not understand why I felt that way for no apparent reason. And then there was the pain . . . the emotional pain made my bones ache, my muscles weak and warm tears stream over pink skin.

It was a perfectly normal day; there was no trigger and yet I was inconsolable. The teacher in the red lipstick told me – as discreetly as you can in a situation like that – to go to the bathroom, wash my face, go to her office and wait there until class was over.

In the school bathroom, I was washing my face for the fourth or fifth time when the school captain walked in, a girl whose heart is a rose, forever in bloom.

'Oh my God, Soph! What's wrong?'

I shook my head like a mad woman. I couldn't tell her what was wrong because I didn't know.

I couldn't thrust a single word over my chapped lips.

Nothing . . . Nothing is wrong.

In the English staffroom, one teacher gave me tea and Monte Carlo biscuits. The others kept their distance and I don't blame them. When everyone is taught to mind his or her own business, it's easy to look the other way.

The teacher with the red lipstick arrived in the office and sat down at the desk beside me. She had been my English teacher for several months and was the fiercest woman I have ever known, and yet the most compassionate, most loving mother to each and every one of her students. She was honest; at times *brutally* honest, and she was both beautiful and brave. She kicked you up the backside if you were slacking off, and she made you fight hard for her praise but boy did she *care*.

'Okay,' she began, 'so what's going on?'

'I don't know.'

'Well something is, look at you.'

'Nothing.' *Crying.* 'No reason.' *Sobbing.* 'I don't know why I feel like this.'

With a broken voice I went on to tell her how I had been suffering from depression but that I hadn't felt this bad, nowhere near this bad before.

'Are you seeing someone?'

'I go to the school counsellor.'

'Okay, well you obviously need more help. This is your HSC year, you need to go on medication before it gets any worse. This is a *very* important year.'

I nodded and blew my nose into a tissue.

'I'm serious. Where is your family doctor? Do you have someone who can take you? Mum? Book the appointment as soon as you get home, okay?'

I almost felt embarrassed because here was this incredible, valiant woman and there I was, a soup of tears soaking into the staffroom carpet.

The late afternoon sun was piercing the room with orange light. The heat on my back made me itch.

She asked me if I wanted to kill myself. I said nothing.

She told me that a year and a half ago, her nephew had committed suicide. He would have been three years older than me. Her face told the rest.

'Your parents gave you this life, it is a gift. It's not yours. It's not yours to take away. You don't have the right to destroy your life. You will break your parents and they will wonder every day for the rest of their lives what they could have done to save you. Okay?'

By this point the lump in my throat was so painful that I couldn't speak; I just nodded to every word, imagining how Mum would break into pieces. I imagined the way someone attempts to glue a vase back together. It's never perfect; you can always see the cracks.

The teacher took my hand. 'Look at me,' she said, 'I know what I'm talking about, I saw it in my nephew and I've seen it in my best friend. She has bipolar and I've even had to be the one to call the ambulance and have her scheduled.'

Although I did not appreciate her lesson at the time, she made the tragedy of a premature death *real*. Her words became a mantra to roll over my tongue on bleak mornings;

something I could cling to on dark days; a war cry to carry me into battle.

．

At the beginning of March 2011, I stopped caring. It's one thing for a teenager to have little care for school or house rules; it's another thing altogether to not care about your own life.

Soon after that, I stopped being scared . . . of anything.

When you have no concern, and no fear to level your judgement, there's an awful lot that can go wrong.

The walls of my rational mind caved in. The bones that had held me together crumbled. My skeleton was dust in the wind.

At the time I had a licence and a car, and a sudden lack of respect for both the vehicle and the road. I would burst into tears at random, sometimes crying hysterically in agony, sometimes crying hysterically with ecstasy. The thick tears would distort my vision like heavy rain on the windshield and I would keep driving.

Several times, when I was agitated by excess energy, I would drive up to a road that cuts behind the Northern Beaches through the bush. There I would drive at 100 kilometres per hour or faster, and see how long I could close my eyes for. My longest was thirteen seconds. When I opened my eyes I found that my car had veered onto the gravel in between the tarred road and the bush.

I started drink-driving, and driving while I was high. I never drove at the speed limit. It terrifies me now, what could have happened. Not to me, but to someone else. What I could have destroyed.

I am so incredibly thankful that no one was hurt during those reckless days.

I look at that young girl and see how selfish and incredibly stupid she was. I have to remind myself, it was not *me*, it was an illness grappling with my mind, making me think, feel and act in that reckless way.

I have the rational ability now to recognise that that behaviour was dangerously wild, yet it's strange because I can still remember how it felt to be that girl who didn't give a shit about anything.

●

I was put on Zoloft to treat depression. The GP said that I would see a difference in three days and would be feeling well again in three weeks.

●

Two weeks before Easter that year I had just finished my half-yearly exams and was about to start my Easter holidays. On the Thursday, a boy who I had been seeing for a month or so admitted that he was still having sex with his ex. I would have been hurt if I had had the capacity to even feel hurt.

I went into school the next day, laughing like a mad woman to my counsellor, saying I was there to share the latest goss from the teenage melodrama that had become my life.

By this point, the counsellor had bought a kettle so that we could drink tea in his room without him having to go down and make it in the staffroom. It was a cheap kettle and would whistle and shake as we spoke. As he handed me a cup of tea, I told him what had happened, finishing on, 'But I don't really care, he was dumb anyway . . .'

He rocked back in his chair and told me about a boy who his sister had dated who was gorgeous but he didn't know what broccoli was.

'You're right,' I told him. 'It doesn't matter how hot they are . . . they have to know what broccoli is.'

'You can make that the title of a chapter in your next book.'

I'll be dead before I have enough time to write a book, I thought but didn't say.

Later, as I got up to leave, he jumped up and blocked the door.

'*Please* be safe, Soph. I would very much like to see you at school next term.'

7

I Feel Nothing and Yet I Suffer

Our family friends own a house on the south coast of New South Wales that we've holidayed at every school holidays for as long as I can remember. Around the corner at the neighbouring beach, a friend of mine owned a holiday house on the hill looking right out over a sea of sparkling blue champagne.

My family and I were going down there for Easter in the second week of the school holidays. My friend, two of her girlfriends and a few local boys were staying at her house. She'd sent me a text, inviting me down for the first week of the holidays. I can't even remember if I'd said yes.

On the Saturday after school finished I lay in bed beneath my covers for the entire day with my red-cloud eyelids. On the Sunday I was up pacing around the house with itchy skin and racing thoughts. The next thing I knew I was carting half my wardrobe down the stairs and chucking it, along with two surfboards and a wetsuit, into my car. I came back upstairs to get my wallet and toothbrush when Mum asked where I was going.

I told her I was heading down the coast.

'We're not going until next week.'

'I know.'

'Then where are you going?'

I told her I was going to stay at my friend's house on the hill. Mum said no.

I said yes and she said, 'I think you need to calm down.'

Then I walked out the door.

Mum chased me out into the street but my foot was already on the accelerator.

I hate retelling these stories because I know now how gutted Mum would have been, standing on the street in a hot black cloud of exhaust smoke. I hate retelling these stories because I hate knowing how the decisions I made while I was sick deeply hurt my family.

At the house on the hill with the local boys, I smoked weed and flirted.

I didn't respect myself, so why would those boys?

I wrote this in a journal that week:

I feel like I'm not scared of the consequences of anything.

I simply don't give a fuck because I don't feel as if I'm going to be around to pay for them.

When my family arrived, I moved out of the house on the hill and into the yellow shed that all the kids slept in at our family friends' house. Mum was still fuming but she was relieved to see me in one piece and agreed that she would let my impulsive holiday slide, provided I invested my time in our family for the rest of the week.

On that first night, I left everyone sitting round the fire and wrote this in my journal:

The end has become a reality. I am down here with everyone around me and yet no one is hearing me scream. Everything they say sounds so trivial – like it doesn't really matter. They're making me so angry, making jokes about teenagers and beer and growing old. No one knows what's coming.

Mum's friends are asking me what I'm doing when I finish school and I'm sitting there on Mum's lap thinking if I make it. And all the while I'm imagining how people will react to it. How they'll cope without me.

I know my mum will never forgive me.

•

During the two weeks I spent down the south coast, my illness took away another part of me: physical pain.

It was mid-April and everyone was pulling out their winter coats. I was running around with bare feet, in a singlet and shorts. Admittedly I feel the cold less than most but this was something else. I felt *nothing*.

After four days, I had scratches and bruises on my limbs from walking through the bush track down to the beach, carelessly grazing my skin on branches and stubbing my toes or kicking my shins on tree stumps or rocks. I wouldn't even notice until someone would say, 'Shit, how'd you do that?'

I would shrug. 'I don't know.'

'Bloody hell, it's purple and blue, it must hurt?'

'Nah not really.'

I wrote in a journal, *I feel nothing and yet I suffer.*

By the end of the week, I had found my second means of self-harm. I burnt three holes in my hand with matches, then proceeded to burn the holes again and again until charred skin wrapped around gooey pools of bloodied flesh.

I desperately wanted to feel something. Anything.

It was strange; everyone looked at the holes and went 'OOH! Ouch!' and then stepped back a little. No one asked what had happened or how I'd done it. I don't think anyone wanted to know the answer.

My family and friends were scared of the unknown; they were scared of me.

I lent Mum's car to an unlicensed friend who drove it up the street past my mum who was walking out of the beach bush track.

When the car was returned Mum screamed and yelled at me in the front yard and I just stood there. It was the strangest thing to know I'd fucked up, that I should feel guilty, but to experience no emotional or physical sensation.

I was meant to be going into town that night for a party but was no longer allowed. I argued back, telling my parents I would go anyway.

'Don't you care? Don't you have any respect for us or our things?'

'No.'

My parents stopped screaming. Mum waved her hand in disgust and walked inside.

Dad shook his head. 'You should, Soph . . . You should care.'

'I know I should! But I don't. I don't care about anything!'

Looking back now, I can only imagine how he would have felt to hear those words spat from his daughter's mouth.

People say you shouldn't care what people think about you and talk about how good it is to be carefree but it's bullshit. *Not* caring devastates the people who love you.

·

Flames wrapped around a pit of logs and dried gum sticks that night when Mum, with a few beers in her belly, told me that the boy who'd two-timed me with his ex was a dick and that I didn't need him . . . as if my heart was broken and *that* was the reason I'd been acting out. I burst into tears.

The conversations around me shifted from casual banter to the kind of 'talking for the sake of talking' that arises in an awkward situation.

'Come on.' Mum took my hand, her beer in the other, and led me up to the house where we sat down on the veranda.

When I returned to school three days later, I had typed up an entry from my journal about the conversation that took place on the veranda that night. I printed it off and when I knocked and found that the counsellor wasn't at school yet, I slid the paper beneath his mauve door before my first class.

He caught me later after my English lesson had finished. I'd already seen him through the classroom window standing in the corridor, waiting for the bell to ring . . . waiting for me.

I asked how long he'd been there for.

'Ten or so minutes.'

'Why?' I asked, and then made an inappropriate comment about him stalking me.

'I wanted to check on you.'

I swung my arms out as if to announce to the world, 'Well here I am!'

'Shh . . .' He waited for me to lower my arms then spoke softly. 'In all honesty, after reading this,' he held up my note, 'I came to check that you were still alive.'

He told my maths teacher that I would not be attending my next class and, instead, took me into the pale blue room, sitting me in the sun on the green couch. I read the note back to myself while he made me a cup of tea, not really appreciating the severity of my sentences.

These are the journal excerpts that I had typed up, printed off and slid beneath his door that morning:

The Moon rises, orange in the east

Burning a hole in the black skin of the night

Burning holes in me . . .

The black skin of the night

This depression is killing me. I don't know who I am anymore. It will destroy them; it will destroy them all. I am so fucking selfish, they don't even know what's coming.

It's one thing to feel okay during the day – to be coping as I move through time.

But it follows me into my dreams now. The erratic emotions, the sudden tears, the vomiting, the nausea, the pills, the confusion, the tightening of my body, the claustrophobia, the desire to escape, the inability to breathe.

We were sitting on the veranda, Mum and me, and she was giving me this motivational speech about being my own person and not letting anyone else dictate my emotions. She told me I needed to forget about him because everything I need to do for the next few months in my HSC year is on me. I can't be relying on anyone else for comfort or protection.

I told her that I don't care about him; I don't care about anything. 'I'm fucked up! It's in my head and I can't get away from that; I can't just forget about it because it's in here.'

(I started pulling at my hair.) 'In here, Mum!'

I told her I needed to escape, and when she asked where to, and I sat silent, she said, 'Do you think about that? Is that something you're planning?'

'I never could . . . it would destroy everyone.'

'Well thank God for that!' She spat.

By this point my face was soaked with tears and my hands and lips were shaking.

And then she started to cry too, sobbing: 'Because it would destroy me.'

I don't even have words to describe how this felt. I think it was the first time my heart had ever really ached.

Georgia and Dad came up and Gee burst into tears . . . I never see Gee cry.

Mum asked her 'Are you okay?' and she said, 'Yes, it just makes me so upset to see Sophie like this.'

Like I said, I have no words to describe last night.

My heart just fucking ached.

Then Mum started talking about how we all love each other . . .

And she was speaking in the same way she used to when I was home sick from school and she'd bring me a cup of lemonade and a plate of Jatz crackers coated on top with soft butter and Vegemite.

She was sobbing but said how 'we all have to support Soph through this'.

I guess it's the first time she's admitted I am actually going through something . . . The most important person in my life has heard me scream.

Afterwards Mum gave me a massive hug and then I went and kissed Georgia, who was still crying, and held her for a really long time. Her body shuddered and her tears dampened my shirt.

I'm the reason she's crying, and then I'm standing there trying to comfort her for pain I've caused. Like kicking someone in the shin then sitting and holding ice to their bruises . . .

Then Mum walked over to Gee and hugged her. They didn't say anything, they just cried and I suddenly imagined that this is what it will look like when I end it.

I'll be free and this image will be real.

I think my heart broke last night.

How can I alleviate my pain, knowing my pain will become theirs?

Please, please, please, please, please, please make it stop.

My counsellor in the pale blue room had bought me a box of Lipton's Cranberry, Raspberry and Strawberry tea. Handing me my mug, he said, 'Careful it's hot.'

I can't drink hot tea; normally I make at least a quarter of the cup cold water to cool down the boiling berry blend. During those grey months, however, the tea would scald my mouth and throat and I would hardly feel a thing. I think we were both hoping that tea and conversation would be enough to fix me and that the pink liquid would restore colour to my cheeks.

'I was really worried after reading that . . .' he told me, blowing on his cup of English breakfast tea with its light milk and spoon of sugar. 'In fact, I'm almost surprised that you're even at school, let alone going to class.'

I laughed. 'I'm surprised too.'

8

My Silent Warrior

I n the six weeks after returning home from the south
coast, darkness saturated the sky and I sank beneath the
surface of a deep, murky sea.

The lack of respect I had for myself resulted in my third
and fourth forms of self-harm: sex and drugs.

I'd made a $100 bet with a friend that I wasn't going
to drink alcohol until the end of the year, and I remember
feeling like I'd cheated him because I was going to be dead
in a few weeks anyway, so I would obviously win.

But although my blood was sober, I inhaled thick smoke.
I turned up on boys' doorsteps at four in the morning like a

cat caught in the rain – sad desperate meows that continued until I was let in. Other times I turned up on their doorsteps at four in the morning flaring, already half undressed. Whether it was comfort or sex I wanted, the merciless way they'd consume me, then toss me back out onto the street before sunrise seemed like something beautiful.

Around this time I was having my first psychotic delusions and I believed that those nights with those careless boys were the greatest, most passionate love affairs to have existed in the history of mankind.

I had lost my virginity when I was sixteen, when my illness was in its early stages. He was older than me and I remember feeling like I was a confident, seductive temptress who had conquered his crown. I thought I'd made the 'dickhead' vulnerable, that he was going to give up his beloved pursuit of women for me, because I was so great and wonderful, because I was worth it . . . because I was *enough*.

There were no clouds the night I lost my virginity, and a thousand silver freckles decorated the night sky. When I walked out onto the street the next day, with my shoes under my arm and my hair a mess, I looked up and the sun burned my eyes. The stars were gone.

It wasn't so glamorous after all. I hadn't been a temptress. I'd been used by a boy who would tell his friends, laugh and then never speak to me again.

I'd never known what it was to be in love, which made it easier for my mind to entertain these delusions about lust and chaos and heat and worship. With the inability to feel physical pain, and the inability to rationalise, my body was battered black and blue. In a bed, in a shower, in a car they could toss me like a rag doll and I wouldn't tell them to stop because I wouldn't even realise that I was grazed and bleeding.

I thought that these relationships were desperate, raw love, and I knew I was going to be dead in a matter of weeks anyway . . . I was manic and I became obsessed with sex, believing wholeheartedly that the love affairs I was involved in would have poems and sonnets and movies and books written about them for hundreds of years after I died.

In a journal I wrote:

Sitting in your ecstasy

Gasping for air

Hot dark rain

This is the moment you will agonise over. You'll want desperately to run back and forth over this page, reading these words again and again.

This is the moment you'll cling to because it's so perfect. He's so perfect; you're so perfect.

You never want to move.

Never want to wake up.

Never want to be alone again.

Your jaw shakes violently because you know you'll be gone in a few days . . .

And so you won't let anything tarnish this moment.

This moment. *Because right now, your senses aren't starving, your skin isn't shrinking. You can breathe. You've become yourself in your purest form.*

You're not surviving. No, in this moment, in loving him, you have survived.

Blissfully manic orgasm and hysterical, agonising depression – sensations at opposing ends of the spectrum – were exactly the same.

For neither can you scream quite loud enough . . .

•

There is a huge mirror on the wall in the bathroom I share with my sister at my parents' house. I came home from school on a Wednesday after I'd snuck out to one of those boys' houses the previous night. I'd been to school that morning for fifteen minutes before telling my teacher I needed the bathroom and coming home. I filled a bath and got into it in my uniform. An hour or so later, when I got out, I stripped myself naked and noticed a line of bruises down the centre of my back. I was quite skinny at this point and the bones of my spine stuck out considerably. It was as if the top of each bone had been painted; some even had the skin grazed off. I stood there looking at them for a really long time and the scariest thing is that I wasn't worried. I didn't see them as coming from an act of violence . . . I saw them as if they were a daisy chain; only the petals were black, green, purple, yellow and blue. I remember thinking my string of flowers made me beautiful.

At the time, someone told me that if you snort heroin, you inevitably overdose.

In many ways, that's exactly what I did with those boys beneath those cotton sheets.

Line the powder on the table. I removed my clothes.

Roll a dollar note. I removed his clothes.

Snort. I inhaled as he entered me without mercy.

I overdosed on bad love.

•

By May I was meeting the counsellor in the pale blue room daily. He would drink English breakfast with skim milk and sugar and I'd drink the berry blend. We'd sit there and talk, desperately trying to fix me.

I began walking out of classes. I couldn't sit still, I couldn't stand the noise, I couldn't stand the itch. In the end I didn't even walk into the classes, I'd just turn up on his doorstep and he'd let me in, sit me down and turn on the kettle.

•

I found my fifth form of self-harm when my skin became so tight that my vomiting could no longer alleviate the tension.

I had made a mess of one arm before my fifteen-year-old sister caught me. Again, I made her promise not to tell anyone.

Growing up, I had always been the leader and made all the decisions for us. My sister had been shy and submissive, but she loved me unconditionally, so as I toppled off my throne, she picked up the crown in a desperate bid to protect me. In her own way, she fought for me every day.

When Gee caught me cutting myself for the second time, she held back tears as she went through each of the bathrooms in the house and took each of the razors out of the vanities, put them in a lunchbox and hid them from me.

I vividly remember coming home from school early the next day just so I could pull apart the house and find the lunchbox. Knowing what I'd done as soon as she got home, Gee tended to my wounds and then reclaimed the box.

It makes me sick to know that, as she bit her lip to stop it from shaking, I made her promise, *again*, not to tell anyone.

A few days later we were at a surf club presentation night when I snuck into the toilets with a blade in my hand and an agonising sadness sitting in my stomach. I was hyperventilating, crying, and then I tore my skin open. My sister noticed I'd gone and came looking for me. She heard my sobs and looked over the door to find me bloodied in the cubicle.

She cried that night, begging me to come out of the bathroom. When I did she took the blade, threw it in the bin, then wet some toilet paper and held it to my skin.

Mum walked in a few minutes later. I can remember feeling so obsessed with my means of 'self-medication' that, even after Mum walked in, I was still desperate to keep it a secret, wanting no one to take it away from me. I had no sense of reality and as Mum's body swayed and she asked, 'What on earth's going on?' I looked across at Georgia as if to say, *don't you dare tell her.*

It's insane now to look back and see that I was so unwell, I forced my sister to keep a secret so massive, and so painful, from my parents for months.

I gave Mum some pathetic excuse as to why I was bleeding and Georgia cried, 'She's lying! She's cut herself!'

Mum asked if this was the first time and Georgia said no and Mum shot the messenger.

'She asked me not to tell anyone!'

'Well don't you think this is something you should have told me? Don't you think I should know about this? She needs help!'

None of Georgia's words made sense beyond that point, she was hysterical.

I'm sorry, Gee, my silent warrior.

I'm sorry that you fought for me for so long without words.

I'm sorry that you carried that nasty secret all by yourself.

I'm sorry that you were scared.

But most of all, I'm sorry that I wasn't taking care of you the way a big sister should.

We left the presentation and, upon arriving home, anything and everything that I could possibly use to harm myself was hidden away. My parents decided not to send me to school the next day. Instead, Dad brought his drawings into the living room, and worked from home so he could supervise me while I sat and watched TV.

That afternoon, I went upstairs and found Georgia's sewing scissors and can remember the way she almost threw up when she arrived home that day and learnt that that's what I'd used.

Dad was angry at the situation. He was angry because he was scared and he was angry because it was his job to watch me and he'd fucked up.

He was angry with me.

At the medical centre, I cried out as he yanked my cut arm.

'Well it's your own bloody fault!'

My dad was angry because he cared so, so much. He was angry at the part of me that was hurting the skin of the daughter he loved.

The following weekend we went to a relative's house and I stole a razor. It was as if I was a junkie. I would hallucinate that my skin was shrinking and I would crave the drug that would satiate me. When I returned home, I hid the blades in different parts of the house and noted their locations in my journal.

My most vivid memory of that time is the sensation of cool, damp undies. I began cutting my hips. The blood wet and stained the fabric.

We have a laundry chute and I remember chucking the undies down and hearing Mum sobbing in the laundry hours later as no amount of Napisan would bleach the tragedy.

•

I have scars.

Scars that have faded from deep red to pale pink petals; scars that turn purple when I'm cold.

I don't like the way some people see them and read the lines like the title on a book cover. I don't like the way some people assume what my story will be before introducing themselves.

I don't find these scars ugly. They do not embarrass me. If I were to resent the scars, I would resent the events that led to them. That much negative energy would chew through my bones. I accept my scars in the same way I accept the illness. For me, it's the only way to move on, it's the only way to live.

I fell into the abyss . . . My scars are evidence that I survived.

•

I went back to school and between classes or on my way home, I started driving up to Long Reef headland. I would climb the fence and sit with my legs dangling over the edge. I felt as though I was living on borrowed time. It was as if every day I was still breathing was some sort of miracle.

There wasn't a huge gap between the fence and the edge of the cliff and halfway down the ochre wall was a ledge where a boulder jutted out from the cliff face. I would sit there and think of how many running steps I would need to take to fly out far enough to clear the ledge and guarantee landing flat on the reef beneath.

Every time I sat there, I would picture my little sister's face, holding onto the colour in her cheeks, the curve of her smile, the bliss that underpins her laugh . . . I would trace those details in my mind again and again until I climbed back over the fence.

Each time I sat there, however, the picture of her face faded a little. It became harder to find . . . harder to hold on to.

Until one day I couldn't see her face at all . . .

9

Suicide

There was an afternoon in early March 2011 when I came home from school at lunchtime, stripped off naked in the backyard, and got into the pool.

I was floating on the cool surface, looking up at the trees. My ears were underwater; all I could hear was the exchange of air in my lungs and the drum of my heart.

I lay there floating for a long time before my naked body slipped beneath the surface. I didn't even notice I was sinking until I was lying flat on the bottom. The silence wasn't scary, nor was it beautiful. It just was.

An entire moment passed where I didn't think I would get up.

That afternoon was the first time I told myself that I was going to escape the disease. It was while standing there, dripping wet on the pool tiles, that I truly started to believe the only way I was going to escape was by suicide.

.

For me, suicide was desperation.

I first understood what it was to feel desperate when I was fifteen and spent New Year's Eve in hospital with scarlet fever.

I'd contracted a strep throat on my birthday. Five days later I woke on Christmas morning with a forty-degree temperature. On the 27th I had a spotted rash around my glands. By New Year's Eve, my skin was scarlet.

I'd had chicken pox and I'd had insane swelling from bee sting reactions, but neither compared to the itch of this rash. At one point you couldn't see an inch of creamy flesh on me; the rash was *everywhere*. It was in my nose, beneath my eyelids, in my ears, on my tongue . . .

The rash lingered for days into the New Year, even after the fever symptoms subsided.

Then one night, the violently scarlet spots near my armpits where the rash had first started began to fade. The next morning, however, I woke to find new spots on the palms of my hands and the soles of my feet.

It hurt to walk; it hurt to hold or pick up anything.

I cried hysterically and Mum came running downstairs. 'Baby, what is it? What is it?'

I showed her my hands, 'There's more! It won't go away, there's even more!'

Her body loosened as the panic drained from her limbs. 'It's okay, come here.'

'It won't go away, Mum, I want it to go away.'

She took me in her arms; stroking my hair, she soothed, 'It's okay, be patient; it's going to go away soon enough, I promise.'

Two years later, she would take me in her arms, stroke my hair and ask me to be patient. 'It's going to go away soon enough, okay? I promise.'

In my journal I wrote:

What's the point in fighting depression when it bites me at any given second? The venom, the poison . . . it seeps back in.

Please, please, please make it stop!

I can't keep fighting.

I don't want to be alone anymore.

At the time, those words were real. I meant every one of them. I was desperate. I was living a nightmare.

I was seventeen and being tortured by a mental illness.

I don't look back now and think that I was exaggerating. I can remember exactly how I felt . . . I was really hurting. The agony, although felt in the mind, was real.

Patience.

At the time, the thought of another second in that hellhole seemed impossible . . .

•

In my journal in May 2011, I wrote:

I wish I could disappear and have no one grieve my absence.

Undoubtedly the three most catastrophic things about suicide are the desperation of the person, the finality of death, and the oily smear of devastation that stains the lives of those who are left behind.

My highs and lows made me incredibly self-centred. *Everything* turned inwards, and yet I still knew my death would annihilate my family. The most twisted thing is that I hated them for that.

I wanted so badly to rid myself from this world – to escape the thoughts that swam in the sour pools of my mind; to silence the whispers of foul ideas; to stop my skin from shrinking.

I wanted so, so badly to go to sleep and never wake up.

I knew, however, that what I wanted (in that sick state of delusion) would destroy the people who loved me.

The deeper I sank, the more they told me they loved me . . . as if I had forgotten.

I never forgot, and in hearing those seven words, 'You know we love you, *so much*' over and over, I only felt guilt.

I wanted to tell them that I wasn't strong enough, and that I was really sorry but that I just couldn't do it anymore. I wanted to tell them that it wasn't their fault. I wanted to say, *please don't hate me; please forgive me.*

But I couldn't . . . I couldn't bring myself to say anything. I don't think there are any words to say when you steal yourself from a loved one.

No words will ever suffice because your loved ones will probably never understand why you stole their treasure and threw it in the sea.

What's more, they'll never stop wishing they could somehow fish you back from the deep.

They'll never stop wishing there was something they could have done to stop you.

They will never stop wishing they could have revived you themselves.

And I think that's why I hated them. I knew I had nothing to say to excuse myself, and so I was stuck. I was bound to this earth by the guilt of knowing my deliberate death would destroy my family.

I wrote in a journal in the weeks before I attempted to take my life:

I have not forgotten how much they all love me,
I have not forgotten how much they all care,
I have not forgotten how much I am valued.
No. I have not forgotten.
What they don't understand is that I resent them,
I resent their affection, I resent the way they beg me to get better.

I resent their love because knowing the agony they are about to experience riddles me with guilt . . .
Guilt denies me my escape,
And so I am left to suffer.

•

During the month of May, lucid moments were like snowflakes.

They were rare . . . pretty, delicate shards of ice landing on the palms of my hands.

They were moments I watched melt on my skin, helplessly.

•

My intention to die truly took hold when I lost respect for the ocean.

Since I was a child I had known the way the ocean could ravage coastlines, sink ships and steal lives. I had known the immense power of the unfathomable blue body and I had approached it with both admiration and caution.

When my mind deteriorated, however, I no longer felt fear. My movements were bold and arrogant. I ignored the vulnerability of my body beneath the sea.

In the week before I tried to abandon my life, I had snuck out and slept with a boy. I lay in the wake of our passionate love for no longer than a heartbeat before he whispered, 'You should probably go now.'

I drove home in the dark hours of the early morning, believing that the real loves, the *great* loves, are intense and painful because lust tortures us. That's why they're glorious – that's why I could only stay for minutes after, because otherwise it wouldn't be dangerous and beautiful and delicious and hot . . . It would be safe, and real loves aren't safe. I believed real loves aren't happy and pleasant, real loves are when you love someone so much you hate them.

I've always marvelled at the way in which our world is darkest right before the dawn. It must have been around 3 am when I was driving home that morning because the night sky was black velvet.

I was driving past Long Reef golf course, with the windows down and the May wind screaming in my face, when I pulled off the road and down the driveway to the beach. I parked in the middle of the car park, oblivious to the white-lined spaces. The wind smelt of winter, and yet I felt nothing of May's chill as I stripped naked and began crossing the sand dunes.

I walked out across the sandbank, and then waded with the dark water lapping around my hips before diving into the deep.

It wasn't until I was out of the water, twenty minutes later, and walking up over the sand dunes and into the white glow of a streetlight that I looked down and saw them. Blue bottles.

There were two or three small ones tangled around my abdomen like mermaid hairs; there was a ridiculously long one wrapped around my thigh; and my hands, feet and legs had red welts from where blue strings had touched but not stuck.

I'm allergic to blue bottles, they make my glands swell and ache. As bizarre as it is to admit now, I stood in the car park with the tentacles drawing blue lines on my skin for several minutes before peeling them off.

I stood there, with blue bottles making my armpits and groin swell and ache, and did nothing. I didn't even panic. I did nothing because in those cold shadows, I liked the way I was feeling the heat.

•

Towards the end of May, I don't think I opened a book at school for the right reasons in any of my classes. There was one day in English where I was wearing elastic bracelets that went into the shapes of different animals when you took them off and I spent the lesson making a play pen for the animals with paper and coloured highlighters. Later in maths, I wrote three pages of automatic writing. My friend sitting next to me scrunched her eyebrows when she tried reading the first few sentences.

In history, I quoted everything the teacher said that *wasn't* related to the course. He was a great teacher but surprisingly his outbursts decorated a whole page. In art class, I was sitting in the park across the road smoking a cigarette.

In the end, being at school, and sitting in the pale blue room drinking tea, was more of a 'put your uniform on and we'll tick you off' type exercise because it meant I was kind of on the right track.

·

Sitting on the green couch, staring at the pale blue walls, with the wind screaming through the quadrangle, I was silent and still.

'What do you see?' the counsellor asked.

Nothing.

'Can you see tomorrow?'

No.

'Can you see yourself walking out of this room?'

No.

It was the first time I had ever been caught in a white-out.

Frozen on the edge of a mountain, unable to see my hand stretched out in front of me. It was the first time I experienced the terror of absolute nothingness. I couldn't see *anything*. It was as if I was unable to tell if my eyes were opened or closed.

With a face wet with tears, I told him I was already dead.

.

On the headland, I'd just sit and smoke cigarettes and cry and watch the sun burn, and trace the details of Georgia's face behind my eyes until I climbed back over the fence.

I wrote in a journal:

I just wish something else would take me . . .

A bus when I cross the road,

A fever,

An infection,

Something, anything, they would deem out of my control,

An accident,

Something that would relieve me of this agony; something that would do the honours for me,

That way they couldn't blame me; they would not judge me for giving up and throwing in the towel,

They would simply accept that I'd lost the fight to an impossible opponent; they'd accept that it wasn't my fault I died,

That way, they wouldn't see me as selfish,

They wouldn't hate me,

They wouldn't hate me for leaving them because my death wouldn't have been my fault,

I'd be free

That way, they'd miss me . . .

And may even smile when they remember my name

When I stood on the cliff's edge on the night of 27 May 2011, the guilt of knowing I would rip their hearts out when I jumped hadn't really gone away . . . it was simply that the desperation finally overrode the guilt.

I paced back and forth to the ochre clay edge, judging the run-up. In the distance, the sun had set behind the hills. There was an intense smoky orange aura above the black silhouette of the earth that made it look as if the world was on fire. There were white caps that raced like wild horses across the grey windswept sea and icy tears in my eyes. The autumn gusts rose up the crimson cliff face, tearing at my hair, beating my face and screaming in my ears.

Over and over I would draw back to the anchor of my breath, focusing on the expression that would twist Gee's face upon discovering that her big sister had abandoned her.

It was a tug of war between this life and the next and soon there were holes burnt in my skin, smoke in my throat and wet tobacco in my cigarette.

I was standing barefoot on the red dirt patch between everything and nothing, and suddenly there was no face behind my eyes to pull me back to safety. It was the most terrifying moment in my life, and yet I wasn't scared in the slightest.

I had intended to throw myself off for weeks . . . The only real difference this night was the way in which the desperation blinded me entirely. I kept trying to picture Gee's face, and my mum's and my dad's, but it was as if I was looking up at them from underwater. I couldn't see the sandy freckles sprinkled across my little sister's nose that would soon turn pink. I couldn't see the sapphire sea in my mum's eyes that would soon cloud over. I couldn't hear the way in which my dad chuckles at his own jokes.

All I saw was an end.

I saw a deep sleep . . . a state of *nothingness*.

I saw rest.

I saw escape.

I don't think I necessarily saw myself going to an afterlife. I simply saw an end to the ache of depression and the itch of mania.

I'd escape my mind . . . it would be silent, and still.

I was blind in believing I'd be free.

But I didn't succeed. Someone saw me; I was saved.

I was so goddamn lucky.

In many ways, the worst thing I remember is being admitted to hospital thinking, *Fuck, they caught me; I missed my chance, now I'll never be free.*

•

No one wants to talk about suicide. That's half the problem.

The other half is that when people do talk about suicide, it often sounds like this:

It's just selfish; it's weak . . .

Or:

It's just a phase; it's for attention; she's just saying that . . .

Most people who talk of suicide aren't taken seriously, until they attempt to make sour thoughts a reality . . .

Without someone to talk to, a thought can very easily become a crisis. When someone is desperate, an impossible idea can snowball until that person starts to believe it is possible . . . An awful, misguided idea becomes reality . . . Death becomes the answer.

I thought death would be my salvation.

I thought that the silence and emptiness of death would be better than where I was.

But I was wrong.

Rediscovering happiness was like a flower blooming on a tree that everyone had assumed was dead. It was better than *any* of the things that death could have ever been.

10

Sweet Sour

I was admitted to a psychiatric hospital in May 2011, and spent two weeks in the intensive care unit. I then spent an additional six weeks on the general ward. I would like to say that in that time I had an epiphany of some sort, and knew all the answers, but what I experienced was far from an epiphany.

While in the ICU, all I did was sleep, eat, go to the bathroom and sip a cocktail of drugs that made me sleep some more. My mind was navigating its way through an alternate reality; my body was turning wounds into scars.

I was also struggling to process delusions whereby I thought *everyone* hated me. I thought my doctor was out to get me, and believed that the nurses were bitching about me behind my back.

It was only really in the days before I was moved onto the general ward that I started to come to terms with the fact that I was still here, living in this life, and not dead, in the next.

•

In all honesty, during those two months in hospital, I absorbed the cocktail, but not a lot else.

My skull was a bone cup filled with cloudy water.

•

When my phone was permitted, messages from close friends filtered through the hospital walls. The most notable was from the man in the pale blue room who sent me a picture of the golden orb rising over the horizon of a blue winter sea. In the text beneath he wrote, 'The ocean is still here, as beautiful as ever, just waiting for you to come home.'

When I put my phone down, I cried and cried because the horizon was so far away and I didn't have the slightest idea about how to get there.

•

My admission was about containment. It was the immediate response to a crisis. I'd been caught in a terrible storm and hospital was the makeshift shelter in the community hall where you go for a temporary bed and hot meals. It was about keeping me safe in the short term. It was about keeping me alive.

It wasn't really until I was on the general ward that I began to talk to other patients. My voice was not as proud, and certainly not as daring, as it once had been, but it was better than nothing.

I began to interact with those around me in the hospital and they helped me write two bold words in my story: 'sweet sour'.

This notion of sweet sour first took root at the nape of my neck when a woman mistook me for her daughter. I was sitting in an outdoor area with a group of women around a glass table. I was holding a foam cup, sipping on cloudy apple juice during breaks in conversation. I remember the still shadows and the dim light on the wall, and the way my breath caught in my throat when the woman next to me turned and took my hand. She had blue veins, painted nails and smooth palms that smelt of rosewater. And then she looked me in the eye, and spoke to a girl who didn't exist in my body.

The moment was so raw; her words were naked and vulnerable. We were all reduced to laughter because it was so devastating to watch her slide in and out of moments of lucidity.

I think it was the first time I truly recognised the beauty in a foul moment. It was the first time I witnessed a magnificent flash of lightning that made me cry with tears of both heartache *and* joy.

The moment was so empty and sour that laughter was all that remained of the real world. Our laughter was so inappropriate and yet it was deep and rich and made our stomachs ache. It was sweet because a residue of beauty can always be found in moments of tragedy. That's what hope is.

I started sitting in the outdoor area whenever I had the chance.

I remember recognising that almost all the trees around the outdoor area weren't native because they lost their leaves to the winter winds. There was one tree, however, that I would sit and look at for hours every afternoon. It had red leaves that outlasted the winter. In one journal entry I wrote:

The wind screams at the sun
As its light bends around the building
To stand as a backlight
For the tree on the green bridge
The scant red leaves
Turn a sour
Yet brilliant
Blood red

One night I was sitting outside with five women. The oldest was a sixty-five-year-old and I was the youngest.

It was winter and everyone was rugged up. For a long time I looked at the creamy outdoor light, melting on the surface of my milky tea. A nurse was standing at the door because one of the middle-aged women had been having heartbreaking episodes for two days. I wasn't saying much; I was just listening to their tongues wrap around stories of distant places and distant lives. At one point, there was a shy gap between conversations when the middle-aged woman declared, 'I'm fucked up.' She then proceeded to tell us how her husband, who had died seventeen years ago, had visited her the day before, and told her, 'Yes, you're fucked up, but that's why I love you!'

This woman laughed then told us, 'And that's why I love *him*, brutal honesty!'

Another woman in her thirties interjected, 'We're all crazy . . . crazy is beautiful.'

'You're right! And if you're not crazy, I say you're just boring!' The middle-aged woman laughed, raising her foam cup filled with blackcurrant juice. 'We're all going to Rome! And we'll drink wine with our left hands because our right hands shake!'

The surface of my tea rippled as our laughter shook the table. Instead of dwelling on our abnormalities, we were celebrating them and that was beautiful.

We defied tragedy that night.

•

I also met an older patient who was no less beautiful than the butterfly tattooed on her skin.

One day when I was sitting in the group room, a nurse (whom the butterfly lady didn't particularly like) walked in with a set of dentures wrapped in tissue paper.

'Have you got your teeth?'

'I think I would know if I didn't have my fucking teeth,' the butterfly lady said with an air of confidence and her chin held high.

The nurse unwrapped the tissue paper. 'So these aren't yours?'

The butterfly lady lifted her fingers up to touch her gums.

'Oh shit . . . they are mine.'

She took them from the nurse and put them in her mouth discreetly. All the while, she kept her head held high.

Before she was discharged, I drew her a butterfly with a felt-tip pen and purple chalk. She thanked me repeatedly but I knew the drawing would never suffice for the way in which she had flown in and out of my life. She had left a trace of purple dust on my hand from where her wings had fluttered against my skin.

She showed me how to maintain self-respect, class and dignity when suffering from an illness that strips you of your sense of self-worth. She also showed me how to keep your fire alive no matter how heavily it rains from the clouds of depression.

·

I remember being in group therapy when the psychologist said, 'I'm going to read out a phrase, and you have to take turns at giving me one-word responses . . . the first thing that comes into your head. Ready? *Another day has passed but it hasn't been tomorrow.*'

One of the men called out, 'Can *thank fuck* be a word?'

The psychologist was less than impressed, but our stomachs were hot from the bouts of giggles.

Laughter truly is the best medicine. In a muggy room, it inspired hope.

·

I met a middle-aged woman who was manic. I called her the southern aurora because she burned like flares of coloured fire in the sky. She read my tarot cards three, sometimes four times a day and I drew her brightly coloured faces with crayons. I think she liked them because she saw her energy in the eyes of the people on the paper. She Blu-Tacked them all to the walls in her room and I think it made her feel less alone, like there were others there with her in her crazed, coloured world.

She liked the drawings and I liked the way she read my cards. On bad days, it meant I could just sit and listen to the rich stories of each card's angel.

She was tragically high and I was tragically low and yet we had found a good dynamic that made our unlikely friendship beautiful.

The sweetest thing of all was that when she read my cards, she always bent the truth so that the cards only gave a good fortune.

.

I met a man who had had a good job, a good house, a loving wife and three beautiful children.

A couch fell on him. No joke – a couch.

He'd been badly injured, and his chronic pain and lack of mobility had made him depressed.

Depression sapped the love out of his marriage and distanced him from his kids. His family had been torn apart. His wife left him taking the children with her, and he ended up in hospital.

I remember feeling heartbroken, as I tasted the sour flavour of his story. This man, however, told stories of exotic places I had not even heard of. He laughed louder than anyone else and as I was sitting around the table one afternoon – thinking: *A couch! How does he even have the will to stand up after all that he has lost?* – I looked up and saw him pushing a paperclip through the hole where his earring should have been.

'Ta-da!' He smiled and held his hands out, twinkling his fingers. Off the end of the paperclip hung strands of silver foil that he'd torn up from a lolly, wrapper and threaded through the paperclip.

'Amazing!' I told him.

•

Quite possibly the most beautiful character I met in hospital was a man in his mid-twenties who had had a brain tumour removed only a few weeks before. His head had been shaved for the operation, so you could see the pink scar that wrapped from his ear around to the back of his skull. He couldn't open one eye completely due to the swelling but I could still see the ocean tides in his irises.

I mentioned the sea in art therapy and after the session he introduced himself. We had lunch together in the dining room and he told me his story: how he'd been homeless at fourteen and had found his place in the surf. The men in the line-up had become his brothers and the jewel-like sea had become his guardian.

We played Uno almost every day and he laughed whether he won or lost.

One day, however, I referred to him by his first name and he stopped me. 'People don't call me that, only people here. Everyone at home, everyone out in the surf, they all call me CJ. That's what I like to be called.'

'I like to be called China.'

He didn't ask how I'd been given the nickname, he just smiled, 'Nice to meet you, China.'

CJ went home a week later, and when I came up to the ward from the dining room, he was gone.

There was a counter where you could make tea on the ward and a drawer full of biscuits where Tim Tams were found occasionally but eaten quickly. When I opened the door to my room that afternoon, there were eight or so Tim Tams that he'd collected from the drawer over the previous few days, having grabbed them before anyone else had had a chance.

I looked up and there was a 'Get well soon' balloon on which he'd written 'China' with a black permanent marker.

•

Understanding the notion of sweet sour helped me to accept what had happened to me. If I were to mourn the sour chunk of my teenage years spent mentally ill, I would feel bitter grief and resentment. Instead, I have learnt to see and appreciate the sweet moments. I have learnt to recognise the blood-red poppies growing on a bloody mud battlefield.

The last book I'd read before my hospital admission was Michael Ondaatje's novel *In the Skin of a Lion*, which introduced me to the idea that our intersecting lives create a tapestry.

It was only in hospital, while frantically attempting to save and store the story of every remarkable patient I'd come across, that I truly came to understand and appreciate this tapestry.

I would never be capable of staying in contact with all of the people I met in hospital but a thread from each of their lives had been sewn into my tapestry, and mine into theirs.

I was blessed.

Blessed for having known them at all. Blessed that I had taken a detail from our chance encounter that would, in the end, make my life richer and eventually help me heal. But I still had a long way to go.

11

Smears of Oil Paint

I went home for the first three weeks of August 2011.

    I had been home a few times on day leave, but walking into the house with my bags, knowing I wasn't going back in a few hours, was strangely unnerving. By then hospital had become a safety blanket, and when it was ripped off, I suddenly felt the cold once more.

    I think the thing I was most scared of was the responsibility because the onus was on me to stick to the schedule, take my meds and, most importantly, not self-harm. I was scared of the part of me that was *not* myself . . . *would I be able to stay safe during an episode?*

I'd been to the therapy groups and met with the doctors and the psychologists, but it seemed that when I had my episodes I stopped being me and became something else.

I wrote in my journal the day after I returned home:

It's true, the roads curve in the same fashion,

The colours melt together in the same way they always have,

And the smells, the tastes, the sounds, greet me as if I've never left.

And so I'm standing there, stunned and silent,

As I realise the only thing that has changed is me.

During those three weeks, I finished my English major work and my Visual Arts major work, which consisted of six oil paintings.

I painted, I ate, I wrote, I took pills and I slept.

I remember crying a lot because my hands shook so badly from the lithium I was taking that the finer details I was so used to perfecting on canvas with my brush were almost impossible to execute. Smears of oil paint turned up on door handles, on the floorboards, on bath towels and on my bedsheets.

•

I began seeing a psychiatrist three times a week. In his room, there was a yellow haze, homely furniture and a red Arabian rug. Although I did not know it at the time, he was a character who would soon shape chapters of my life.

His smile was forgiving, and he had milky blue eyes that disappeared beneath wrinkles when he laughed.

He was a man, honest and wise, with a beard as white as snow, who would save my life . . . again and *again*.

Right from the beginning I trusted him. Maybe it was his gentle nature, or maybe it was the fact that he saw something in me – something that was terribly wrong. He saw me lying on the seabed, and made every effort he possibly could to fish me from the murky drink.

Within minutes of us meeting he had sighed, leant back in his chair and said rather quietly, 'You're in an awful lot of pain, aren't you?'

I'd nodded as tears welled.

'I don't think anyone has really understood how much you've been suffering.'

I remember the surge of hot, salty water as it flooded the red plains of my cheeks.

His words were the most profound thing anyone had ever said to me.

Major depression had not yet been identified as a misdiagnosis, but he did help to explain the numbness I had experienced earlier that year. He told me that when you suffer from intense emotional pain, the mind tries to protect you by suppressing that pain in the subconscious. It is a conversion disorder that causes patients to suffer from neurological symptoms referred to as '*La Belle Indifference* – The Beautiful Indifference'. In other words, it is a psychological form of self-defence. Most cases stem from trauma. Mine stemmed from the emotional pain associated with my illness. My case, however, was not as extreme as blindness or paralysis. Instead, my mind had protected me from my own sour thoughts and feelings by making me numb.

He had then called in my mum and explained things in a way no one ever had. It meant everything to have someone vouch for me. Yet while his words validated my pain, they crippled Mum. Her body had folded in her chair.

In the car park afterwards, she said to me, 'Don't worry, baby, okay? We're going to do everything we can to fix this.'

I couldn't say anything; I just burst into tears. Then as we'd pulled out of the driveway into the white haze of a streetlight, Mum started sobbing too. For the entire trip home, the radio was barely audible beneath our cries.

It wasn't until we were halfway home that I looked across at Mum and noticed her hands. I had never seen fingers shake so violently. She could hardly hold the wheel.

Other than leaving the house to see the snow-bearded psychiatrist, I only ventured out, over the next few weeks, with Mum when she needed to go grocery shopping.

I'd forget to shower and would go for a few days before Mum would realise and turn on the tap. I think that was a mix of the underlying depression and the cocktail of drugs. I forgot who I was; I forgot *what* I was.

12

I'm Sorry I'm Not Her

It was in the thick of winter when dark rumours were passed among my peers. Two friends who I'd loved and trusted first uttered the words and within days the comments had festered.

It was said that I was a fake and was making up my illness for attention. It was even suggested that I had been staying in a hotel, not a hospital.

I found out through social media and it tore me open.

Shaking a little, I stood up from the computer and told my parents I was going to get changed into my pyjamas.

Upstairs however, I bypassed my bedroom and retreated to the bathroom.

I tore *myself* open.

I had barely been home and I was already being admitted for the second time. Mum sent me a message on her way home from the hospital saying *I miss you already.*

I remember feeling so guilty because I knew how badly she wanted her little girl home and I knew I couldn't fulfil her desire. I was sick.

Mum and I fought a lot during that admission.

I was seventeen and legally didn't have to have her in my meetings. She hated the hospital, because she loved me and she hated me being there. She hated the hospital and the doctors and the psychologists because they had taken me away and were yet to fix me.

Ultimately, I think Mum hated the fact that she couldn't fix me herself.

One day in particular, I was so exhausted I was wishing I were dead, and Mum visited saying she wanted to take me out on leave and go for a walk. I had an hour sign-out and we walked down the street to a café. The entire time, I was saying how I wanted to go back and go to sleep. I stopped multiple times on the footpath and it took several minutes each time to coerce me into continuing the walk. I was so depressed that the mere act of placing one foot in front of the next was agonising.

'Don't you want to be outside? Look at how sunny it is! Don't you want to be out here in the fresh air and not in . . . in *that* place?'

She couldn't understand that I didn't want to be anywhere; I didn't want to exist – I simply didn't *want*.

And who could blame her?

What mother *wouldn't* find it impossible to understand why their child no longer wanted to live?

Mum was angry because she loved me so much but had no control. She was helpless, and yet her anger made me stressed. No matter how many different ways I tried to phrase the answer, no explanation was adequate. At the time, she couldn't see, and I couldn't make her see, so I shut her out.

In hindsight, I realise she was terrified but I was fighting battles in my head every day. My attention had turned inwards as I fought to silence my enemies; so I had very little energy for anyone else.

Mum and I fought bitterly; it was a muddy tug of war. But eventually, we found each other in the middle.

·

The greatest thing I learnt from my second time in hospital was to distance myself a little from others – in particular, other patients.

I learnt the benefits of receiving smaller portions of detail with regard to other patients' stories as well as sharing smaller portions of my own. There is only so much you can digest and if you consume the problems of every other person you meet, there is no room for you to address your own. I learnt to empathise with other patients and share small portions of my story that applied to theirs without overwhelming myself with the weight of each person's plight.

There is great comfort to be found when you confide in someone who understands and shares your grief but trouble arises when you neglect your own fight to attend to theirs. The tapestry you weave has to be yours – not a replica of theirs.

•

In September 2011, after almost four weeks in hospital, I came home.

For three months, I lived in the shadow of my mum. I was her dark silhouette, and although I did not appreciate it at the time, she was my crusader.

She fought for me until she was beaten black and blue – and then she'd swing her sword again. My mum was ruthless and relentless.

I owe her everything.

At that point I was seeing my psychiatrist with the snow beard three times a week. I would then see my GP once a fortnight to make sure I had all the right prescriptions. I also saw a naturopath once a fortnight. After meeting with her, Mum and I would drink miso soup. It was a salty treat that reminded me of the late February sea.

After I'd been home for a few weeks, Mum started her sun-kissed campaign. She'd force me out of bed every day at nine. Most days, it would result in screams and tears as the nasty cocktail of drugs I was on had me waking each morning with a wretched hangover.

Mum would wait for me to take my meds, bring me out to the dining table, place a bowl of nuts and seeds with homemade almond milk on the table, before blending up a thick green smoothie. After that she'd hand me my clothes and shoes. We'd argue and I'd cry because the morning fog was yet to rise above my eyes, and my skin was tight, and a deep sadness sat like acid in my stomach. I'd tell Mum that I didn't want to live anymore and ask her over and over why she was making me.

But then she'd swing her sword again, fighting until my shoes were on and we were at the beach car park. Then she'd fight until we were halfway down the beach, and when I sat on the sand crying, she'd fight until we'd made it to the end.

'See, I told you you'd make it.' She'd smile even though her lips were trembling.

In early November, Mum started doing casual work again. I would go with her into the office and she'd try to ignore the way the other staff members looked at her as she walked in with a seventeen-year-old zombie in tow.

I was her shadow under the desk.

For two weeks I sat on the floor beside her with my earphones plugged in and my laptop on my knees, making a video with a bunch of photos and an accompanying song. When it was done and I showed her, she bit her lip as tears welled. She knew exactly what it was; I'd made a memorial video for my family to play at my funeral.

.

The few weeks of late spring and early summer that year were among the lowest I experienced. My moods were not as volatile as they had been earlier in April and May, so I wasn't really experiencing those intense waves of devastation. Instead, I was a vegetable. I cried a lot and I laughed at nothing. I was sipping on a fruity cocktail of drugs that made me black out for hours at a time, I had no energy and I was numb in every sense.

I was a vacant stare, and that's truly no way to live.

I remember reducing my dad to tears, telling him just to let me go, because his daughter was already gone. I told him I was just the shell of a girl who no longer lived inside.

I honestly believed that.

I wrote in a journal:

I don't know if I'm angry with them for trying, or if I just feel sorry for them as they grieve.

'I am already dead!' I scream at them.

'That girl you loved; she's not coming back; she's dead. And I'm sorry I'm not her. I'm sorry I can't bring her back to you, but she's gone . . . You need to accept that.'

I owe it to my family for never accepting those ill words.

They admitted I was lost, but they refused to stop searching until I was found.

•

Speaking with my mum recently, she told me that loving someone who didn't love her back was the hardest thing she's ever done.

My mum had been fighting for a daughter who refused to fight for herself.

I asked her why she'd kept fighting.

She told me that even if I'd forgotten who I was, she hadn't.

When I was a baby, Mum walked the length of the beach from Collaroy to Narrabeen every day with me on her shoulders. When I grew old enough to walk, I'd trail on the sand in her shadow. Now, Mum persisted in getting me out of the house and to the beach to walk because that was where it had started. On the cool, wet sand between the land and the sea, that was where we had always been.

She told me that depression had sapped the love and affection from beneath my skin. In loving me, however, she knew that eventually I would remember how it felt.

Like I said, I owe her everything.

•

For the better part of October, I was so heavily sedated that the hallucinations of my skin shrinking were contained to some extent. November, however, was a different story.

I started having obscene urges that I would obsess over for days.

I wanted to break my left arm and I knew exactly where I wanted to break it, and how I wanted it to happen. A week later, I wanted to cut off my breasts. No reason exactly, I just craved it in the same way you might feel hungry and crave a deluxe Portuguese chicken burger.

Mum had the knives locked up for three weeks.

It was mid-November when we were driving home from the man with the snow beard's room and I heard 'Never Let Me Go' by Florence and the Machine on Triple J radio station for the first time. For about a month after, I was convinced that the song had been written for me and that I had a personal letter from the singer explaining how she'd been so touched by my story that she'd written this song about my journey. I was frustrated for days because, no matter where I looked in the house, I couldn't find the letter.

The song became the soundtrack for my funeral video.

November was also the time in which I started hearing things. Not things like strangers' voices whispering in my ears. Instead, I'd hear things like Mum calling out for me to pull the clothes out of the washing machine. Then I'd stand at the machine dumbfounded when I raised the lid and there was nothing inside. Mum would walk in and ask what I was doing and I'd literally be scratching my head saying, 'But you just asked . . . ?'

On one occasion I was sitting at home with a girl with golden locks and I started rambling an answer to her question, spewing sloppy sentences onto her lap, before she stopped me. 'What are you talking about?'

'But you just asked me . . . ?'

'No I didn't,' she said in a grave tone. 'I didn't say anything.'

I then started having what my psychiatrist and I were calling false memories, when I would imagine something to have happened or would imagine something someone would have told me and take it to be a memory. I lost my ability to sort fact from fiction.

All I can say is that when you're a teenager trying to find your place in the world, suddenly finding yourself unable to determine what is real from what isn't is incredibly distressing.

Thankfully, I had people around me who were points of reference in the real world, people who made sure I didn't lose myself altogether.

•

I started dreaming, and not the way a sane person dreams.

When the average person wakes from a dream, the details are foggy; most things don't make sense . . . Who was that random person and where did they come from? How did we suddenly get there?

The boundaries of space and time don't exist in the average dream the way they do in the real world. There are loose ends and jumps in time.

For two months, the average dream became my reality. I was living in the real, physical world with everyone else and yet the details were foggy, and most things didn't make sense. I was awfully confused nearly all the time.

My dreams became the world in which I lived.

I would be awake each day for nine or ten hours, waking up at nine every morning and going to sleep by seven every night. I napped sometimes during the day as well. The boundaries of time collapsed and the hours passed quickly. During the night, I could live for up to three or four days.

There were several nights where I lived for entire weekends during my sleep. I went somewhere on the Friday, spent the day there, woke up on Saturday, ate breakfast, lunch and dinner with activities in between, then woke up on Sunday morning, ate meals with activities in between and then *actually* woke up in my own bed in the real world feeling exhausted from the imagined weekend I had just experienced in my dreams.

The details in the dreams were clearer than those of the real world. I would be able to sit in my psychiatrist's room, describing the completely fictitious worlds with their unique cultures and landscapes as if I was not just describing my suburb but the entire city of Sydney.

I had names for all the imagined places in my dreams, and at one point I visited the same great lake in four different dreams. On one side of the great lake was a city and suburban area and on the other side were fishing villages and farming areas. In two separate dreams I spent time in the city, once in someone's apartment, and another time I had dinner in a restaurant at the top of a luxurious hotel overlooking the water. A week later, in a third dream, I was staying in a house on the water in one of the fishing villages on the other side and was looking back over the lake to the giant skyscraper hotel. I turned to someone and said, 'I had dinner there the other night.'

'Really? What's it like?'

I smiled. 'Incredible.'

The fourth dream I had, I was on a thirty-two-foot yacht sailing on the lake for two nights. I remember standing on deck, looking at the city lights, then gazing back to the faint glow of the fishing villages.

When I told the man with the snow beard about the fourth dream at the great lake, after having spoken about this place in three separate sessions, he scheduled me for an MRI, saying he didn't want to alarm me, but it would be good to rule out a brain tumour.

•

I went back to school for a few days in the last week of term. Despite having once been social and confident, I found it difficult to navigate the schoolyard. I felt like a novelty, like I was a quirky toy won at a circus.

Mum dropped me off and picked me up as if I was in kindergarten, which was certainly warranted on the third day when I left the school grounds.

I had been walking down the hall towards my classroom when I heard two classmates reiterate the rumours that I was a fake and had made the whole thing up for attention. Beaten by the words, I ran down to the gates before anyone could see my tears exploding. I don't really remember what happened next all that well, but one of my friends saw and came running after me. She took her jumper off and held the sleeve to my face to stop the blood that was now seeping from the slices in my cheeks. She asked me, 'What did you do this with?'

I held up a piece of rubbish – a crumpled soft drink can.

She didn't say anything, she just held me as we baked beneath the sun until my body stopped quaking and the blood on my cheeks dried. The counsellor thanked the girl who had chestnut hair when she delivered me to his room. She kissed me, and left.

He sat me down to talk through my distress. 'Tea?'

•

By mid-November, everyone in my year group had finished their year 12 exams. They were boarding planes, kissing in the tropics, partying until sunrise and lounging by sparkling pools.

I was at home . . . an injured blue bird in a cage.

I remember crying because my peers were alive and I wasn't. In hindsight, I needed that time alone because it gave my broken wings time to heal.

Later in December, our ATAR scores came out.

When I'd started my final year of school, I'd told Mum that I was going to get a score of ninety-eight per cent. I'd written it on a piece of paper in black bold texta and stuck it to my bedroom wall with Blu-Tack. My family had asked me if there was a course at university I wanted to get into with this mark and I'd said, 'No, I just like the number.'

In the days leading up to the release of the scores, having missed almost fifty per cent of the required school days, Mum reminded me that I needed to be happy with a score in the 70s or 80s, and that with the year I'd had, getting an ATAR at *all* was an achievement.

A thick blanket of depression lay over me on the morning of the results. Mum got the letter out of the letterbox and she and Dad came into my bedroom to open it with me.

'Remember, what's important is that you made it through the year,' Mum said.

I opened the envelope. My score had been estimated from the half-yearly exams I'd sat before my first hospital admission. My two major works had also been taken into consideration. It was 98.25 per cent; I had top bands across every subject, and was receiving a NSW Premier's Award for All-round Excellence.

I said, 'Cool', handed Mum the piece of paper and rolled over to go back to sleep.

.

I think my eighteenth birthday rocked me because, for almost a year, I had been sure that I wasn't going to live to see the day.

I was still delusional, severely depressed and feeling my skin tighten on occasions. For me, 2011 had been chaos. I'd spent 365 days beneath violet clouds where the wind screamed and the seven seas roared. I was washed up and exhausted.

The New Year arrived and brought with it a third hospital admission.

I had met a boy in late December who was everything that I *had* been. He was intelligent, philosophical, he loved the ocean, he was an explorer craving new lands, and he was a painter. Above all, he was free.

I didn't tell him I was in hospital. Instead, I pretended I lived in the suburb where the hospital was, which failed as a lie when he came to take me to an art exhibition and found he had to come in and sign me out.

At this point, I'd been taken off the anti-depressants to be reassessed and was nearing the end of the medication detox. I intrigued this boy, so he signed me out for a few excursions. He told me how he'd dressed up as a snow snake for New Year's Eve, and I laughed.

The snow snake was a breath of fresh air.

He said, 'If you had to choose, what is the one phrase you would live by?'

I told him, 'One crowded hour of glorious life is worth an age without a name.'

'I like that.'

'Me too.' I grinned. 'What's yours?'

'Buy a ticket, take the ride.'

'I like that.'

He smirked. 'Me too.'

Our friendship was entirely platonic, and he was good for me because he didn't baby me. He saw a mind that could be salvaged. He heard a voice that still had something to say.

During this admission, my mum bought me Khalil Gibran's *The Prophet*. During the first week of the medication detox I felt so nauseous I couldn't focus my eyes on the words. As I sobered up, however, I found it easier to read. I ended up reading the book three or four times, highlighting sections to read to the snow snake when he took me out on leave.

We would discuss the various philosophical quandaries, down at the sea baths. It was there, sitting on ocean rocks, dipping our feet in the blue harbour drink that my mind began to resurrect itself.

Gibran's work made me think a lot about life. For the first time, I understood joy and sorrow to be two parts of the same thing and could appreciate tears of heartache and tears of happiness rising from the same well. I also considered ethics on a global scale and was reminded of the great change I had wanted to instigate as a fifteen-year-old girl with the world at her feet.

I began thinking about how I wanted to live my life and in contemplating the infinite possibilities of my existence, I started thinking about *why* I wanted to live my life.

And although that life was still incredibly fragile, it was such a beautiful thing to see a future.

13

The Cocktail

The first time I hallucinated about my skin shrinking in hospital, a nurse came into my room with two cups – one cup of water and a second cup with a pressed yellow powder pill.

I was crying hysterically, my shrinking skin was red with blotches and little beads of blood from where I'd been scratching it, and my hands were shaking violently as she watched me put the pill on my tongue. She then held the cup of water to my chapped lips, rubbed my back and soothed, 'This will help it to pass . . .'

I woke up eight hours later.

The nurse was a voluptuous woman who called me 'goddess' and herself 'the supreme goddess'.

I was so confused looking out my window at the night sky when I hadn't even eaten lunch yet. 'You've been asleep for quite a while, almost nine hours! Feeling a bit better now?'

I couldn't bring myself to say anything.

She took my hand and held nail scissors to my fingers. 'Don't worry, this won't hurt.' Her gaze dropped to my crimson-grazed skin. 'We don't want you doing that again.'

I hadn't had my fingernails cut short in a long time and so it felt weird having my pearly pink nails trimmed right to the skin bed.

The supreme goddess assured me, 'Dinner will be up soon, I ordered extra in case you didn't like what I'd picked.' She had a heart of gold, lime-green eyes and pink lipstick, and yet I remember sitting there, wanting my mum.

It was the first time I had ever been sedated.

It hadn't made me feel better, it had simply made time pass. I had skipped forward nine hours.

In the year that followed there would be more time travel than life spent in the present.

•

I spent my first two weeks in a psychiatric hospital in the Intensive Care Unit on suicide watch. I was allocated a psychiatrist and a psychologist. Not every patient gels with every doctor and while I don't doubt the highly qualified expertise of either of them, I soon found flaws in the way they approached me as a patient, as a human being.

The psychologist would linger awkwardly because unlike the subtle, constructive critiques of the man in the pale blue room, I felt like her words were those of a textbook.

The psychiatrist I had would dart in and out of my room at random. His words were limited – not because English was his second language, but because, in my opinion, he didn't empathise. I felt like I was just a room number on his checklist. What's more, he was always asking me nine questions about side effects for every one question about my actual emotions.

'Do you have a rash? Blurry vision? Dry mouth?'

'Nope.'

'Okay, good, we'll increase the dose.'

My pills were little yellow and purple caps, and because at that stage everyone thought I had major depression, the more he filled my glass with this passionfruit cocktail, the more intoxicated I became.

I was spun out; my words slurred together.

The anti-depressants made me worse, and when the doctor saw that I wasn't getting any better, he made the yellow and purple caps larger and their delivery more frequent.

Within five weeks, as a fifty-five-kilogram seventeen-year-old girl, I was on the highest possible adult dose of the medication. My 'episodes', however, continued. I was still hallucinating that my skin was shrinking, feeling it tighten around my bones, which resulted in those yellow pressed powder pills, that had first knocked me out for eight hours, being administered more frequently. Slices of pineapple were thrown into the blender.

The problems with those anti-psychotics, however, is that you build an immunity to their sedative effect . . . so the dose increased.

The larger pills were pink pressed powder – I was given them to sleep at night. I was also given oval pale-green slow-release ones at breakfast and lunch to stop the hallucinations and erratic behaviour during the day.

The drugs I was taking were becoming an icy blend of passionfruit Passoã, pineapple vodka, strawberry champagne, pear cider . . .

I remember the first night I took one of the pink pellets. I had had an awful afternoon. I was acutely suicidal, two chunks of pineapple had failed to sedate me, and so the supreme goddess entered with a white paper cup with the pill and a foam cup of water. I swallowed the pink fruit drink, with Mum sitting beside me on the bed patting my back, and my best friend sitting on the armchair with her legs kicked up onto the desk.

It was before 7 pm but the nurse advised Mum that it was getting late and that it would be a good idea to help me start getting ready for bed. The supreme goddess unlocked my cupboard so that I could get my clothes out and waited until I was changed so that I could put my dirty clothes back on the bottom shelf. Then she let Mum take out my toothbrush and toothpaste before she locked the door.

As I turned to face my friend, I couldn't tell if she was moving or if it was the room. I took a step forward and slammed into the wall. Mum caught me by the elbow. 'You all right?'

Her words echoed in that beige cave. The next thing I remember was falling between my room and the bathroom, burning my knees on the carpet. I crawled while my friend laughed, telling me how fucked I looked. Her laugh was empty – the kind of laugh where you just don't really know how else to react. Mum hoisted me up onto the toilet and I sat there, slumped awkwardly against the tile wall of the cubicle, while she brushed my teeth. I remember being in that bathroom, with the white light burning one of my retinas, as I watched, through one half-opened eye, four people move in front of me – Mum and my friend.

It was that clichéd scene from a trashy teen flick that went straight to DVD where the sloppy young protagonist has had too much punch at the party, and has been taken home by Mum, who holds her hair back while she vomits, before Dad enters the bathroom and grounds the girl for being drunk . . .

Towards the end of my third week on the general ward, my doctor told me my depression was resisting treatment, and prescribed another medication to help the anti-depressant to work. It was supposed to enhance the effects of the anti-depressants.

The new pills were pressed powder as white as coconut flesh that I initially took on a medium dose at night, which became a high-night/medium-morning dose, which then became a high-night/high-morning dose.

Caribbean coconut rum *enhanced* the cocktail.

It made my hands shake.

A girl with oak skin lent me a bottle of her lavender nail polish when I was on the general ward and, although it doesn't seem like a big deal now; I was reduced to tears when the purple glossed more skin than nail. I was a painter, and the medication had stripped my hands of their talent.

My cocktail of drugs was a tropical drink that was supposed to quench my thirst, but it only ruined my nights.

The worst thing was that I stopped being able to hold conversations because I would forget what I was talking about halfway through.

I have always been very articulate, with a clear voice and a sharp delivery; it's something I pride myself on.

My grandpa, a human encyclopaedia, is also very articulate. I grew up listening to words that I had not yet learnt roll off his even tongue. Mum often jokes that my skull, like his, is larger than most because our brains need the extra room.

When I was eleven, my pa had a stroke, and then another when I turned fifteen. Both times, he had to learn to talk again. I remember being in the hospital, after his second stroke, with my sister holding up a kids' book with words like 'cat' and 'boat'. He tried to connect his mind to his tongue until his eyes were red and bulging and his face a juicy plum. I felt so sorry for him, but it wasn't until my own tongue became dry that I truly understood his plight.

Mum had cried when Pa spat words that didn't make sense. Her eyes watered again when I threw a book at the wall because I couldn't deliver, 'No thanks, could I have wholemeal instead?' without forgetting what the question was mid-sentence.

As it had been for my pa, to find myself unable to hold my own in even the most basic conversations was heartbreaking.

The hallucinations stopped for a while, and my episodes became somewhat less frequent. I became a bit less suicidal; I ached a bit less; I cried a bit less. My depression became slightly more tolerable but that was because I wasn't really *there* to experience it.

The party I was at was fucking shit, and sipping on that fruity drink didn't make the party any better. I'd wake up every morning hungover from the cocktail of drugs.

I'd lie there dozing until a nurse woke me up for the third or fourth time, before trudging down to the nurses' station where I would receive yet another foam cup.

I'd be drunk again within the hour.

•

The more toxic the cocktail became, and the more of it that I sipped through my swirly party straw, the less of a person I became.

Later, after that first admission, I asked my doctor with the snow beard why people black out and can't remember getting home when they drink too much alcohol, yet still manage to get in a taxi, spit drunken words into the driver's ears, pay for the ride, stumble up the driveway and find their bed.

He told me that people in that state can carry out ordinary, mundane tasks because they're on autopilot. They function on their most basic level, but their brain is not actually recording the information, so they don't commit their experiences to memory.

I have little memory of my experiences between June and December 2011. I was functioning on my most basic level. I was on autopilot.

I was *there*, sitting beside you in the room, but I was not a person. I was not Sophie Hardcastle.

During my second admission to hospital, another medication was added to the mix in my liver. Peach pressed powder, to further enhance the effects of the passionfruit anti-depressant.

·

The cocktail silenced my soul. It clouded my mind such that I would sometimes forget my words altogether; I'd just stand there mid-sentence, with my mouth hanging open and my tongue dry . . . Blinking as if I could somehow open my milky blue eyes to the end of my sentence.

The strawberry champagne, coupled with my lack of mobility in the hospital, caused me to gain nine kilograms in four months. Having always been exceptionally fit and healthy, this caused me much distress. I already saw myself in a terribly ugly light, with depression having warped my perception of the contours of my body, the pink in my cheeks and the curve of my smile. The weight gain only intensified this dirty light and I was no longer proud of the body I had always thrived in.

I had been very confident in the past but my new shell, my depressed feelings of low self-worth and social paranoia, combined with my inability to hold a conversation, made me terribly self-conscious.

The first time I went out at night with friends was two months after my second hospital admission. I went to a friend's house and we were planning on walking down to a casual bar on the beachfront near her house. Six of us slaved in front of the mirror for hours, perfecting our makeup, our outfits and our hair. Then there was time spent choosing the right shoes and the right bag to tie it all together.

It was a big deal for both my family and me that I was there. In the three or four weeks before that night, several friends had taken me out from beneath the protection of my mum. They would try their best to make me feel like we were hanging out the way we used to, but no matter how hard they tried to disguise it, they'd become my babysitter.

That night with my friends was no different. When people know that you want to hurt yourself, even end your life, very few people are willing to let you out of their sight.

One of my friends offered me a burgundy lipstick. I pouted while she painted my lips with the blood-red pigment. Then watched as she fumbled through her makeup bag for another stick and coloured her lips scarlet.

I was wearing a black lace dress that somewhat concealed the weight gain and, as I gazed into the mirror, the lipstick made my irises glow like the water of an ocean rock pool at dusk.

We arrived at the bar around eight-thirty, an hour before my dad was coming to pick me up. I wasn't eighteen yet but there wasn't any security at the door.

I'd *loved* going to parties before, even ones where I only knew one or two people. I'd loved the wealth of stories that I was yet to hear. I'd loved my own air of mystery. I'd flirt and laugh and make conversation to the steady rhythm of my pulse.

That night, however, as we entered the bar, my blood was sticky and hot and my pounding pulse was thick in my throat.

The passionfruit Passoã already made my skin turn red at random; so my nerves only intensified the colour of my scarlet freckles. I hovered behind the other girls, like a child hovering behind her mum at a crowded zoo.

Moments later, the girls split to talk to different people and I stood there, suddenly unsure where to place my next foot. It felt like *everyone* was looking at me, when in reality I was faceless in a crowd of drinks, wet coasters, loose change, and peanut bowls. My laboured breath was silent beneath the exchange of cheerful banter.

The next thing I knew, a blond friend swept me up off my feet and I was so shocked by the sudden embrace that I didn't even notice my dress riding up my backside. He put me back down on the floor moments later and a second boy hugged me. 'Where have you been! We haven't seen you in *ages*, you myth!'

My neck was a violent crimson and I remember standing there, with a parched tongue and an empty voice. The boy with scruffy blond hair butted in, 'You're still in year twelve though, aren't you? Have you been studying?'

I blinked. I nodded.

'You nerd!' He laughed, messing up my hair with his hand. 'Come on, I'll buy you a drink.'

'I'm not drinking.'

'Since when?' The other boy interjected.

The blond boy laughed. 'Is this part of your study regime as well?'

I blinked. I nodded.

'Ha! You are such a nerd!'

He took my hand and we walked to the bar.

At the bar, I managed to say, 'You line up, I just need the bathroom.'

'What do you want to drink?'

'I don't care . . . whatever.' I shot an awkward smile, fled to the bathroom, locked myself in a cubicle and vomited.

My dad picked up on the second ring.

'Can you please come and get me now?'

'Are you okay? Where are the other girls?'

'I'm okay, I just want to go home.'

I waited for fifteen or so minutes in the cubicle before walking out, disappearing straight into the crowd to find the girl with the scarlet lips. 'I'm going.'

'Going? We only just got here!'

'I know, my dad's about to pick me up.'

I said bye and thanked her for having me, then kissed her on the cheek.

I was almost at the door when my dad walked in. I don't think a teenager has ever been so relieved to see their dad walk into a young, trendy bar.

By the time we got home, my cheeks were muddy with wet mascara and the burgundy lipstick was spread across my face like the wide painted smile of a tragic, washed-up clown. I brushed my teeth, had a shower and drank my

fruity cocktail. I was knocked out, asleep on the empty
dance floor before nine-thirty that night.

.

When I was nine, my mum was in hospital for a week with
a throat infection. She was still very sick when she came
home, although she'd been prescribed numerous courses of
strong antibiotics. A friend of hers told her about a GP who
specialised in alternative medicines and, as Mum's body
failed to respond to the antibiotics, she decided to pay this
woman a visit. The doctor took Mum off the antibiotics,
gave her alternative natural remedies to sweat out the nasty
infection, and changed her diet to ingest rich vitamins and
minerals. By that point, Mum had been seriously ill for four
weeks. After seeing this doctor, she was significantly better
within four days.

In October 2011, after my two lengthy hospital admissions, Mum took me to see the same GP. At that time, Mum
was desperate. She was dragging around a daughter who
no longer looked like her daughter and no longer sounded
like her daughter.

The doctor was a general practitioner, but she was also a
naturopath who studied and practised Eastern remedies. She
was holistic, and often spoke of the arrogance of either Eastern
or Western practitioners who assumed they knew all there is
to know, when she believed you had to learn both disciplines
to know where each of their strengths and weaknesses lay.

Her foyer and consulting rooms were purple. She wore purple, her furniture was purple, her pens were purple, her walls were purple – *everything* was purple.

And then there was her. Her skin was as gold as the sun. She was the epitome of health, and she radiated light.

The golden woman recognised within minutes that the cocktail of drugs was depleting my body's nutrients. My body was suffering from the medicine that was prescribed to heal my mind.

She wasn't my psychiatrist so she couldn't tamper with my medication. Instead, the golden woman did everything in her power to help my body metabolise my medication better. She turned the cocktail into a green smoothie – literally.

I woke every morning to a green smoothie with four different types of green, leafy vegetables, two other vegetables, and four different types of fruit. I stopped eating wheat and dairy. My animal protein intake was also limited to three times a week. I ate a breakfast bowl of seeds, activated nuts and sliced banana with nut milk. For lunches and dinners, I drank miso soups and ate raw salads or tempeh and brown rice.

The cocktail of medications I was taking in 2011 had the potential to reach levels of toxicity in my body if they were not metabolised, or 'flushed' out properly. The golden woman believed dairy and wheat products were slowing down my digestive system, so my body was using up more nutrients to expel the food and medications, leaving me nutritionally deprived and exhausted. She didn't think eating would cure me, but she did think getting me into optimum health would help me have the resilience to fight the battle better.

I wouldn't have been able to stick to the new diet had it not been for the time and energy Mum invested in it. Fighting for me every day, she woke every morning at the crack of dawn to prepare my meals for the day. She then started shopping at the farmers' markets and soon our home was abundant with fresh fruit and vegetables.

The golden lady also put me on nine different types of vitamin, iron and fibre supplements. At one point, with her pills and the ones I was taking from my psychiatrist, I was taking twenty-seven pills a day.

For a while I absolutely resented consuming so many tablets and I would cry most mornings as I shovelled capsule after capsule down my throat. One morning, when I had thirteen different pills and caps in one of my hands and was so sick of funnelling them in pairs onto my tongue, I filled my entire mouth with the handful and tried to wash them down. I coughed the ludicrous amount of pills up and onto the floor while three remained stuck in my throat. Mum came running in while I stuck out my tongue and pointed down my throat, crying as I choked. She refilled my glass of water to wash them down and they started dissolving. The powder inside the capsules burnt my throat such that

I could feel it for the next few days when eating. After that, Mum sat in with me while I took my pills each morning.

I certainly resented taking all that medication but I just had to remind myself that, unlike the party cocktail, the golden lady's pills were like raw pulped fruit juice *without* the alcohol. Her green smoothie was thick and sometimes hard to swallow, but it was exactly what I needed.

I lost six kilos over the next month and a half. My skin shone red less frequently, and in the wake of the scarlet flushes, began to glow. And although I was still very sick, I did have a little more energy.

All of those things meant that I started to *look* more and more like myself, and in looking like myself when I stood before a mirror, I started to *remember* myself.

•

In December 2011, when my brain scan results showed no abnormalities, the man with the white snow beard spoke for the first time of epilepsy and bipolar disorder. It was in the lead-up to my third admission and my mood swings were becoming more pronounced as I fluctuated between states of severe agitation and severe depression. What's more, the suicidal tendencies started to return.

My psychiatrist explained that rapid mood swings are characteristic of both bipolar disorder and, in rare cases, temporal lobe epilepsy. The additional hallucinations and confusion I was experiencing built stronger cases for both possibilities as he considered I was either experiencing the psychotic symptoms of bipolar 1 or epileptic seizures of the temporal lobe.

From my birthday on 20 December until 3 January, I lost myself entirely. I was admitted to hospital on 4 January 2012, so I could be weaned off the cocktail and reassessed because *obviously* the drugs weren't working.

Which made total sense. I hadn't been responding to the anti-depressant medication because I didn't have major depression.

Those first two weeks in January 2012 felt like I was breaking an addiction, and it was cruel.

When the strawberry champagne that knocked me out at night and the pear cider that sedated me during the day were withheld, I lost an additional two kilos in five days. My pink-cloud eyelids were somewhat less puffy and I could ask for the lower dose yellow pills when I really needed them. By that point, however, I hated the way the pineapple vodka affected me so I started riding out the sudden devastation on my own, even though it made me hysterical. It was nice to finally have some control at the bar as to what went into my drink.

It took me three weeks to come off the passionfruit Passoã. Anti-depressants are notorious for their uncomfortable withdrawals and the yellow and purple caps I was taking were notorious for being the worst.

I was on the highest possible adult dose. It was a long way back down to earth.

During this hospital admission, I was agitated and irritated, which made me very unpleasant to be around. I had insane headaches. I was dizzy and incredibly nauseous. Almost every time I ate I would feel so sick that I would vomit. Then my stomach would be rumbling so loudly by the next meal that I'd pile food onto my plate and eat it in a matter of minutes, only to lose it a matter of minutes later.

The worst side effects were the sensory disturbances, whereby I experienced shock-like electrical sensations. When I walked, it felt as if electric shocks were reverberating up my legs to my torso, making me feel weak. When I touched anything with my hands, the electric shocks stung my fingertips, surged through my palms and reverberated up my arms to my shoulders. When I moved my eyes they ached and when I turned my head, it was as if the movement was stilted, the way a dancer appears under a strobe light.

It was a three-week hangover after an eight-month bender sipping on that sour cocktail.

When I finished the passionfruit detox, the Caribbean coconut rum was left on the shelf. Within a week of stopping the rum, my hands stopped shaking. My hands were an artist's hands once more.

Regaining my talent as a painter was another way in which I started to remember my old self.

Peach schnapps was all that was left in my green smoothie, as it was both an anti-epileptic and a mood stabiliser, so whether I had epilepsy or bipolar, it would keep me tipsy until I could go home and see the man with the snow beard again, who would make a decision regarding my future treatment.

In February 2012, with epilepsy testing scheduled and the recognition of distinct bipolar features – such as suicidal depression and the racing thoughts and recklessness of elevated moods – the bottle of peach schnapps was put back on the shelf with all the rest and my glass was topped up with a purple drug that was also an anti-epileptic and a mood stabiliser, and proven statistically in cases like mine to be more effective. The blackcurrant liquor was poured into a small glass, so the side effects were not as chilling – I was no longer the lonely drunk dancer, unstable on the dead dance floor.

The fact that I was actually being treated for the right diagnosis meant the new drink was effective for the right reasons.

What amazed me most was how quickly things changed for me.

By the end of February, in a mere three weeks, it was like watching the clouds part to see the sun again.

There were details that I hadn't noticed when it felt overcast or when I was drunk on the drug cocktail . . . colours I didn't see.

By March 2012, I could finally see the world again for what it truly was. Beautiful.

14

Playing With Fire

When I was around eleven, Mum and I were driving home from the aquatic centre one afternoon. It was only a fifteen-minute drive and yet, as often happened with us, we were in a conversation so deep it was as if we'd been driving for hours. We rounded a bend in the road as Mum told me how she believed every person who comes into our lives is a teacher.

She explained that every character who walks with you through the pages of your story has something to say. Some will share their wisdom by word of mouth; others will lead by example, giving you something to aspire to. Some people will lead by example and show you the *wrong* way to do it; how *not* to live your life.

But whether it's positive or negative, every person you meet has something to offer you. Even if neither of you is conscious of the lessons, wisdom is shared.

•

When I was thirteen, I often Googled quotes. Once I typed in the key word, 'happiness'.

The quote that carved the greatest impression on me was this:

Time spent laughing is time spent with the gods.

When I was younger, I possessed an intense appreciation for the beauty of a heavy laugh.

The raw crack of thunder that ensues a glorious flash of light.

It was only when I became sick that I truly appreciated the joyous clap of thunder amid purple clouds rolling on the black horizon.

Three girls taught me one of my life's greatest lessons. They taught me of the wonders of inappropriate pleasure.

They helped me to adopt the joker's flare, his energy. They taught me to laugh hysterically in the face of my tormenter, and how to free myself from the tyrant's hold.

They rallied behind me, and taught me how to rise above, by giving me the courage to mock my mental illness.

Those three girls are among the bravest people I know.

•

Many people find it difficult to be around those who are sick, especially when the sickness is a mental illness. It pains them to see their loved one suffering. But I also think that seeing their loved one 'out of their mind' or 'mad' reminds them of their own psychological vulnerabilities. As my sanity began to crumble, many of the people in my life felt threatened.

Witnessing the manifestation of my illness threatened them because it reminded each of them of the fragility of their own psychological state. Your mind constructs your reality. Your mind is how you make sense of the world, and so to observe someone who is losing his or her capacity to reason, it destabilises your own perception of a fixed reality.

For this reason, the more my mind fell apart, the more friends I lost.

I don't blame anyone for backing away. My illness consumed me and, in the same way I forgot Sophie Hardcastle, I forgot who my friends were. If I didn't recognise myself then why should I expect them to?

But those three girls refused to walk away. They are among the bravest people I know because they not only crawled into the shadows to see me; they carried a stick that was burning orange, purple and blue. They lit up the small dark cave. They laughed at the tragedy of my situation. They set my world on fire.

One of the girls has blonde ringlets that she hates, but that I love. Her curls are as alive as the blue tides that sway in her eyes. She was one of Australia's best young athletes and yet she is still trying to find her calling. She can chew your ears off with her banter and, even if she is talking shit, it's sometimes all that you need.

The second girl has silky brown hair that somehow can't stay neat for more than five seconds – maybe that's due to the theatrical way in which she moves her body when telling a story. Her smile is wide and infectious and her husky voice is full of charisma. She is intelligent, well spoken, self-disciplined and honest to others. The real reason I admire her, however, is because she is honest with herself. She knows what she wants. She was born to be an actor, and no job application or university pamphlet can steer her from her cause. She does what she loves and she loves what she does.

In many ways, she is responsible for this book.

The third is modest, so much so that many underestimate her wealth of knowledge. She has class, a wide vocabulary, is stunning in any outfit and wears quirky glasses. When she lets down her guard, she's a riot with crazed blue eyes and high-pitched giggles. When she composes herself, she is elegant, and I often wonder if she understands just how wonderful she really is.

Each of these girls could make me laugh.

Together, they made my cheeks wet and sore, and my tongue dry. I'd be unable to breathe – choking on the joke they'd wedged in my throat.

Together, they ignited a fire within that would burn my belly as I laughed uncontrollably. The flames were glorious.

Over and over, those three fearless girls reminded me that I was alive.

What I remember most about hospital visits was the elephant in the room. It was great that my friends and family had taken the time to come and see me. Although on *really* bad days, especially in the beginning, I was often too exhausted or in a mood too sour to talk with my family or even to appreciate their efforts.

People sat on the end of my bed, or on the armchair. I remember their awkward poise. The silence. It was kind of like, *okay, I've come to see you, and now I'm here, and now I've seen you and . . . well, what next?*

I wasn't very good to talk to, but I felt strangely obligated to entertain my visitors, as if they were guests at my house and I had to make sure they enjoyed themselves. When several of my friends from school came to see me during my first admission, I'd often act lively, trying to fill the time. They came with the best intentions but, more often than not, visits were more exhausting than uplifting.

It was a very strange dynamic. Friends and family came to show their love, and it was almost as if I was expected to be welcoming and cheerful because they were there, and they'd come all this way to see me . . . But if I were genuinely welcoming and cheerful, I wouldn't have been there in the first place.

Looking back now, I would just like to say thank you to the loved ones who visited. I would like to say thank you to my family in particular, who came even when I ignored or resented their presence. I may not have appreciated it then, but you were the people who reminded me I had a home and a life to return to.

I can also appreciate that for most it was confronting not only to be in the psychiatric hospital but also to see the body of the girl they knew inhabited by something else. I could see it in their eyes, a grey flicker. I remember the way they'd walk on eggshells as they spoke. *How are you feeling?* Nothing deeper in case they hit a nerve. *What are the nurses like? Can you go outside? What's the food like? I've brought you something to read, something to listen to, something to eat. Do you get bored? When can you come home?*

Premeditated, safe words . . . but please don't think I am ungrateful. People fear the unknown and so it was everything just to have them there.

I've been told that courage isn't a lack of fear; it's having fear, but being able to do it anyway.

I don't doubt that those three girls were frightened, and that is why I am forever in their debt. They were scared of being burnt, they were scared of things they didn't understand and yet they played with fire anyway.

If there was ever an elephant in the room when they visited, their humour would have taken a black marker from my pencil case and drawn a thick black moustache above the elephant's trunk, and we would have laughed at the absurdity.

They relaxed on my bed, sometimes even lying beneath the sheets and pretending to be patients when nurses walked in. They sat slumped in the armchair as if watching TV on a Sunday night. Once, one of them lay upside down in the chair with her face turning pink with blood and her feet tapping up against the wall. If I had energy, they would stay for the hour until the nurse kicked them out. If I didn't, they knew when to leave.

They brought me a large amethyst crystal that was meant to help heal the mind. It was confiscated because I was in the ICU and at risk to myself. For several minutes the three of them begged the nurse to give it back, laughing as they came up with ridiculous excuses as to why I should have it, before being asked to leave.

With thanks to the investment my parents had made in a private health fund, my room in the ICU during my first admission was as comfortable as an ICU room could be. The walls were painted with honey cream and I had carpet. But at the end of the day it was a hospital room and even if you were to adorn it with a thousand wild flowers, it would still be a hospital room, and there is nothing beautiful about that.

I also had a large window; I could see the sky, but the window was sealed shut, and unbreakable.

I wrote in my journal in June 2011, while in the ICU:

I'm looking at the window and imagining the cold winter air,
And then I begin to suffocate, my heart races in a panic,
As if the air in here is no longer real.

For a girl who had grown up knowing the salty taste of a winter's southerly gale, the stale air inside the hospital was the thing I struggled most with. Visitors had to buzz in and out of the ICU and so the only air that came in was through an old ventilation system. Dusty draughts tasted like a life once lived. The rooms were dry, and strangely neither hot nor cold, as if summer and winter had died and this stuffy in-between was all that was left.

The window in the room looked out over a pallid concrete building with big tinted windows. If you squinted your eyes at the building's black glass wall, you could see through to the business offices within. For two weeks, my activities included wandering between my room and the bathroom, which was only twelve feet away; watching *Slumdog Millionaire* in the small common area and sitting on the end of my bed, looking up at the people walking around in the office.

Observing them, I don't think I was thinking of anything in particular – I would simply sit there, like a snowman inside a snow globe watching snow fall.

I didn't talk much. There wasn't much to say.

I didn't laugh either. I didn't laugh in that cream-coloured room with its stale air and fixed window until those three girls came to see me.

Those three brave girls were a breath of fresh air. They carried in the winter sun and the summer breeze. They shared whispers of the real world.

Visiting hours were between four and seven and they arrived the first time around five because they'd had to go home from school and get changed before driving over. As they walked in, they joked about having been frisked for presents or belongings that I may use to harm myself. *Yeah, we brought her a gun.*

From my window we could see the car park exit below the office building. As the girls chatted in my room, cars began to drive out of the car park. They were expensive cars, carrying expensive workers wearing expensive suits.

I'm not sure how it started but I think one of my friends said, no doubt with a deviant grin, 'Let's pretend we're patients.'

Within minutes, the three of them were standing at the window, banging on the glass and pulling crazed faces at the people driving beneath. One woman tapped her male colleague on the shoulder and pointed up at the girls. The pair seemed to exit the car park somewhat quicker than the rest.

I lay there, and watched the jokers dance.

They were asked to leave when the nurse walked in for my fifteen-minute suicide check, and while I cried hopelessly for hours into the night, my stomach still burned from the way in which I'd laughed.

The second time they visited they brought me the crystal. Although grateful again to see them, I was still too tired and drugged up to properly interact. I just sat and watched with a sheepish smile while they laughed and insulted the nurse for confiscating it.

By the time they arrived for their third visit I was out of the ICU and on the general ward. It meant I could go down to the dining area to have my meals. One of my friends was going on about how hungry she was – she is slim but food is her god.

Again the words slipped out with a giggle: 'Let's pretend we're patients.'

The second told us that she'd already eaten, but dared the hungry one to try.

The hungry one had just come from drama rehearsal and was wearing grey tracksuit pants and a black Bonds hoodie. Approaching the serving table, she pulled up her hoodie so it hung over her face and pushed her tray along painfully with limbs that seemed to be failing her.

Her portrayal of the depressed teenager was so ridiculous that I bit my lip to avoid giggling. When she arrived at the staff member who was serving us, he looked at her suspiciously. 'Are you a patient?'

'Yes,' she hissed from beneath the black hood.

'*What unit?*'

She paused, and I waited for her character to unravel.

A moment later, she looked up with an expression so foul, she practically spat in his face, 'Three.'

The man took half a step back. 'Lasagne or chicken?'

My friend looked up at him with cold brown eyes and uttered, 'I don't care . . . whatever.'

We walked away with a plate each of lasagne and salad.

At that stage I'd had three dinners in the general dining room. The walls were red and the lights were cream, creating this strange pink haze as I'd sat by myself.

As I started walking over to a table, one of the girls turned to me, 'Let's eat outside; there's an outside area isn't there?'

'I think so but I'll be cold.' I was wearing a cotton t-shirt, thin leggings and slippers.

'I'll run up and get you a jumper from your room,' the other girl offered.

She was back a minute later with her blonde hair falling out of its bun, a jumper in her hand and pink blood beneath her cheeks.

I remember that night well because, after weeks of tasting the stale breath of the ventilation system, the winter air bit into my lungs and reminded me I was still alive. We sat around a table with aluminium legs and ate, while the three of them joked about the different types of mental patients, hellishly exaggerating false stereotypes.

The darkness that night was thick, but there were hundreds of stars and I realised I'd forgotten how extraordinary it was to see tiny lights burning in the sky.

The jokes those three girls made were so inappropriate. They were offensive. But they were *everything*.

They never asked me awkward questions or tried to tiptoe around the truth. Instead their words were bold; they were brilliant.

The three of them taught me that to laugh at something takes away its power. To laugh inappropriately is courageous because it is defiant.

For a long time my illness crippled me, it controlled me; I became a slave to its cruelty.

And that is why I needed to laugh; laughter sets the world on fire. When a situation is messy and unpleasant, the jokes need to be messy and unpleasant; they almost need to be inappropriate. That is how you rise above. That's how you survive.

15

The Petri Dish

During my second hospital admission, I walked past the nurses' station and heard a woman who suffered from acute anxiety cry hysterically to a trainee nurse, 'Every day I stay in here is costing me hundreds and hundreds more, I can't borrow money off my parents! They don't even think this is a real illness, and my doctor won't let me leave until I'm better!'

The woman's fair skin was plum red, her fringe was stuck to her wet cheeks, and I remember looking at her – as she frantically flicked through paperwork – heartbroken.

As I walked away, I didn't know who was more overwhelmed, the woman or the trainee nurse.

Unlike many children in my neighbourhood, I was always well aware that my life was comfortable.

To have grown up with food in my fridge, clothes on my back, a roof over my head and a place to sleep; I am richer than seventy-five per cent of the people who walk this earth.

To live with money in my own bank account and some spare cash in my wallet, I stand among the top eight per cent of the world's wealthiest people.

Sometimes I felt almost as guilty as I felt grateful.

I thought that I had acknowledged all there was to be thankful for, but there were comforts that lay deeper, like one thing that I had ignorantly assumed was simply part of *life*: private health insurance. As a teenager, this was undoubtedly the greatest luxury that my parents had afforded me and I hadn't just taken it for granted; I hadn't even known it existed.

My parents could not have known I would end up needing hospitalisation and ongoing treatment but their investment in private health insurance bought me small comforts that made big differences in the outcome of my treatment.

It wasn't until I was discharged from hospital for the third time in February 2012 that I realised how lucky I was. Mum was sorting through her accounts and called out for me. I walked into her office and she swung back in her chair, swivelling to face me. She told me that if we hadn't had private health insurance, she and Dad would have had to mortgage the house. She was almost laughing because it sounded so ridiculous.

I stood there, gobsmacked, with my bare feet melting on the varnished floorboards – the floorboards their hard-earned money had bought – and recalled the woman with the scarlet face and the trainee nurse who couldn't get a word in. *What had happened to that woman?*

And then I had an even scarier thought: *What happened to the ones who couldn't afford any medical treatment at all?*

•

People who are underprivileged often cannot afford adequate help to deal with a mental illness. Many have experienced emotional or physical abuse, violence or family dysfunction or have suffered great personal hardships. Society sees many of these people as having a 'reason' for their illness.

Her boyfriend abused her and so there is a reason *she is depressed.*

Yet she doesn't have the financial means to access quality medical resources and so she suffers silently.

For those who are privileged and able to afford help, society often argues there is no 'reason' for you to have a mental illness.

I had grown up in a nice area, gone to a good school, had great friends and a loving family and had been taken on many holidays.

What could she possibly be depressed about?

The help is accessible but there is no *reason* for it and so I had suffered silently.

Those kinds of judgements had quickly dissolved the ground on which I stood. I had fallen through the floor into the abyss.

Look at how great your life is, what could you possibly have to feel depressed about?

I had given no answer; I was silent.

And then in waves came:

Guilt. *They're right, I have so much to be grateful for, why aren't I grateful?*

Shame. *Am I a bad person?*

Confusion. *If my life is so great why do I feel like this?*

Stress. *What's wrong with me?*

People can see a broken leg and can sign the cast. They can see a rash, rub ointment on it and watch it fade. They can hold up a scan to a light box and see a brain tumour. A mental illness isn't visible. I think that is why so many people are reluctant to acknowledge its presence.

I like to think a person with a mental illness is like a person listening to a song through headphones. Their lips are moving because they're mouthing the lyrics. Their fingertips tap their desk, and their feet shuffle on the carpet because they can feel the rhythm.

But those movements don't make sense to someone watching.

They can't understand it because they can't hear the song that's playing.

Does that make the music in the person's ears any less real?

If someone else can't hear the song does that mean it's not there?

•

In the early days of 2011, as the first of my symptoms hatched and swam to the surface, I couldn't comprehend what was happening.

If I couldn't understand it, how could I possibly explain it to someone else?

As each day passed, the battles I was fighting in my own head became more brutal and more violent. I found myself in inner turmoil, and it was exhausting. Each day I grew weaker.

It made it almost impossible to fight any battles that arose outside my mind.

So when those two people who I had loved and trusted told my peers that I was a fake, that I was making my illness up to gain attention and had been secretly staying in a hotel, the walls around me collapsed. I had no energy left to defend myself.

Mum was sitting next to me at the kitchen table while my friends fired abusive words through instant messaging. 'It's fucked,' Mum told me. 'You *cannot* believe this. You know and I know that what they're saying is not real. Turn it off.'

I pushed her away; I didn't want to turn the computer off. I wanted to understand. I wanted to know what had warranted this outburst; I wanted to know how they could have *possibly* come to pass these judgements.

I was crying and when the messaging stopped I stayed at the table for a few minutes with Mum's hand holding my own and Dad's palm cupping my shoulder.

'I'm going to go upstairs and get changed,' I told them standing from my chair.

Mum gripped my forearm, and her glassy dark blue eyes fixed on mine. 'You okay? Their words are nothing, Soph, I promise.'

Yes, I pulled myself from her hold.

'Well, come straight back down after, dinner will be ready soon, we've made lamb, your favourite,' she said. In hindsight, I can hear the crack in her voice. She was scared.

Five minutes later my mum would come to regret letting me leave the table.

I remember the way my skin shrunk, and the way it tore.

I remember the cold tiles.

I remember the burst of light from the ceiling as Gee flicked the switch and found me.

In the two months that I'd been in hospital, I had seen my sister's lip tremor, her cheeks flush pink and her eyes glass. But she hadn't cried in front of me.

I don't think I've ever seen her cry the way she did in that bathroom that night.

She yelled for my parents, and as Dad rushed in I remember her crying to him, 'I don't want her to go back, she only *just* got home; they're going to take her back. I don't want her to go back!'

Dad doesn't have a lot of hair, and as he knelt beside me with a towel, his scalp burned as red as his face. His eyes were soon bloodshot with tears. He was bawling and, as his body quaked, salty droplets flew from his skin and landed on mine.

Mum was the worst; she *absolutely* lost it.

I felt stomach acid rise to the back of my throat, as I watched her heart tear in two. She pulled at her hair, she stomped her feet, she slapped the wall, screaming hysterically, '*NO! NO! NO! NO!*'

I remember looking over Dad's shoulder and watching Georgia thrust her arms around Mum as she bucked like a wild horse in a rodeo.

Despite what I'd done, my body wasn't hurting.

Only my heart was.

That was undoubtedly the cruellest thing about my battles with self-harm.

I couldn't relieve my agony without inflicting excruciating pain upon the ones I loved.

My salvation was their devastation.

I'm sorry! I'm sorry! I'm sorry! I'm so, SO sorry!

No matter how many times I said it, they didn't hear me.

I think that's what grief does; it takes you somewhere else.

.

Looking back, I don't blame anyone for what they said about me. They were young; we all were and trying to find our way in the midst of an unforgiving illness that warps reality.

Much of the criticism stemmed from the fact that I was talking about my mental state and therefore it was assumed that I was *bragging* about it. But the truth is, I have always been extremely open. For one, I am terrible at keeping secrets or lying. For another, I was raised by a woman who believes in honesty.

When people ask me questions about myself I answer them truthfully. I am not afraid to tell people my flaws, my weaknesses, my fears . . . I am not afraid to tell them my attributes, my strengths, my passions. I am not afraid to tell someone who I am.

My mum maintains there is no point in pretending. Lying to others is almost as tiring as lying to myself.

Once I knew what was happening to me, I approached my mental illness with the same philosophy as my mum's. I didn't see the point in denying it or trying to cover it up. If I were to do so, wouldn't I be worsening the misconception that a mental illness is a weakness? That a psychological disorder is something to be embarrassed about?

If anything, I believe that sharing my story raises awareness. People don't know enough about mood disorders, addictions, eating disorders, psychosis, behavioural disorders or personality disorders . . . and so they fear them.

Social taboo silences people; the result is often catastrophic.

Being as open as I am, means there will always be people who will cast a negative light on my words. Telling strangers my story 'must be for attention'. Therefore it 'must be fake'.

I understand that not everyone is comfortable sharing, but I am, so I don't see the point in trying to conceal something that, although it does not define me, is a significant part of who I am.

I was seventeen when those rumours were spread. Like a plague, they infected social media. My mum and my best friend told me not to buy into it, but it spread like a virus beneath my computer screen. The more I bought into it, the more irritation it caused, and yet I couldn't walk away. It was almost as if I too was contaminated by the outbreak.

A few days later, my best friend saw a post online and drove round to my house. She turned on my laptop while I lay in bed beside her with a pounding headache and puffy eyes. I was terribly hungover from the anti-psychotic drug Seroquel.

'We're temporarily deleting your Facebook,' she told me.

She didn't show me the post; I don't think she even told me about it until months later, and even then she didn't tell me what had been said. Both she and my mum decided that Mum would have my phone and that I'd only see messages from my sister, my dad, my best friend and two other girls.

It was the best thing they could have done for me.

At the time, however, I hated it. I so desperately wanted to defend myself against these allegations. People were listening to other people's slander about me and there was nothing I could do to stop it.

My best friend maintained that, if I were to retaliate, I would only validate their claims. She is remarkable; she gave me the strength to silence my screams.

It was an incredibly difficult lesson to learn when to quietly retreat, but the wisdom I walked away with was invaluable.

In the end, to hold onto a grudge would have eaten me alive. Negative energy weakens you. And so I chose to let go. I chose to forgive. I chose to breathe.

•

There were other times when people unintentionally attacked me for being ill. It's amazing how much damage one sentence can cause. A string of words, a series of sounds; that's all it can take to cripple the mind.

Mind over matter.

Three tiny words, one sentence . . . that's all it took to silence me.

I was coming back from the city on the ferry one night with friends a year later in October 2012. We were sailing across black water when one of the boys fished me from the group and reeled me in to a deep conversation. He told me his sister was suffering from an eating disorder.

It was unusually warm for October; the night was dark and the salty mist made the cabin glow beneath yellow lights. My friend started to share his frustrations with me. He was drunk and I was sober, offering a shoulder to lean on. Then he said, *'China, it's mind over matter, like she could just eat.'*

Although I had never suffered from an eating disorder, I had met a lot of beautiful people within the walls of the hospital who had. Talking with them, I'd soon learnt that the greatest insult to the majority of sufferers was when people said 'just eat'. Many of the people who loved them – their parents, siblings, extended family, boyfriends, girlfriends, friends – told them 'just eat'.

If they heard that from the people who loved them, imagine what they heard from the people who didn't.

That night on the ferry, I tried to tell my friend that asking his sister why she couldn't 'just eat', was like asking me why I couldn't 'just be happy'.

The ferry rocked and his eyes widened. His jaw dropped, his hand with a beer in it was raised. 'Exactly!'

I remember thinking, *yes! He understands.*

And then he said, 'You see my point! Why can't you *just be happy?*'

I couldn't speak; I was paralysed.

'I believe in mind over matter, if she *wanted* to, she would eat. If you *wanted* to, you would be happy. Depression, bipolar, anxiety, whatever people want to call it, it's just in your head, if you *wanted* to, like really put your mind to it, you could just not have it.'

I wasn't sure if he was really drunk or just fucking stupid.

'Yes,' I told him, 'this illness is in my head, just like a tumour is in someone's breast, or a rash is on your skin.'

'Mind over matter.'

'Are you serious? I can't make it go away any more than a person with an amputated foot can grow a new one . . . You know, if they really put their mind to it; if they really *wanted* to grow a new foot . . .'

'Mind over matter,' he told me again, smiling.

I bit my tongue, got up and walked away before the tears that glazed my eyes could melt onto my cheeks.

I told my psychiatrist about the conversation a few days later.

'That's *bullshit*,' he stammered.

I laughed because it was the first and last time I ever heard him swear.

His face wrinkled as he started laughing too. 'Seriously, that is absurd.'

He went on to tell me that the mind does not *create* the illness; at best it tries to protect you from it, by suppressing thoughts and feelings in the subconscious.

'To tell someone that if they really wanted to, they could choose to be better,' he said, 'that the mind could just *make* them not have a mood disorder . . . Well, it's just such a dangerous thing to say.'

•

In the first few months that my illness manifested in 2011, my mum couldn't understand what was going on. She couldn't understand why I was falling apart when I had so much going for me. She couldn't understand why I wanted to give up the wonderful life she had given me. Her lack of understanding resulted in fear. Fear resulted in panic.

Above all, her confusion resulted in anger.

She later told me, 'I guess it was the same with Dad' – he had suffered from undiagnosed depression and anxiety for seven years. 'I would just look at him and think, *what could have possibly made you feel this way?* A wife, a lovely home, a job he enjoyed, two beautiful daughters . . . what was wrong with that? It was very hard not to blame myself . . . it was very hard not to blame myself for both of your depressions.'

Her words made my heart ache.

My mum had seen things that I could not even imagine. She had spent her teenage years living in Hong Kong while it was still under British rule. At that time, hundreds of thousands of desperate Chinese refugees poured over the border to escape the bloody Chinese revolution. When she finished school, she moved back to Australia to live a life of luxury in comparison to the many homeless who had littered the streets of Hong Kong. In the year she turned nineteen, a terrible evil devastated her. The pain this evil inflicted upon her left her in pieces on the floor. She was depressed, and it was a long time before she could trust again, or love again, or feel joy again, but she did.

She *won*, because she climbed out of that hole and into the baking sun. What's more, she did it on her own.

She felt that she'd had a *real* 'reason' to be depressed, when I had no 'reason' at all. She'd overcome it herself; she'd managed.

So why couldn't I?

That question had simmered beneath her skin for weeks. It made her hands clammy. It made red blotches appear and oily tears slide down her olive cheeks.

It was not, however, until we were standing in the car park of the family medical practice we'd been going to since I was born, with the naked sun on our necks and a prescription for anti-depressants in my hand, that she erupted and words burst from her body like hot red lava.

'I've had things happen to me, real nightmares. I've had fucked-up things happen to me, but I realised that that is life. Life is messy and I realised that only I could drag myself out.

And I did! I moved on with my life, I lived again. I let it go, I overcame it. I didn't need medication; I didn't take some happy pill. I had a real reason to feel devastated, and I rose above it without some drug a doctor prescribed me.'

Anger, pain and panic spewed from the volcano.

I remember the way she drove home with just that little bit more aggression. The turns were sharper, the accelerations slightly crueller and the braking so abrupt that my chest pressed tight against my seatbelt when we approached a red light. I remember her bloodshot eyes. But, most of all, I remember that my sobs were the only sounds to cut through the thick, awkward silence.

Many people think that medication is the easy way out, like a little red flashing apple in a computer game that you eat to take you straight to the next level. Medication is not a cheat, and the implication that it is 'cowardly' is the reason so many people go untreated.

A doctor does not write prescriptions for every person who walks through their door; instead they exhaust all the possible non-medicating treatments first.

Mental illnesses are caused by biological or environmental factors, or a combination of both. If the patient is experiencing environmental stress – such as a divorce that is causing them to encounter episodes of depression – the doctor and/or a psychologist would employ psychological strategies through therapy to help them cope. If that wasn't enough, the doctor might prescribe medication to temporarily help them manage their emotions until the environmental stress dissipates.

If it were determined that the patient had a biological predisposition to depression, medication is prescribed to amend the flaw in chemistry.

That imbalance of chemicals is real and cannot simply be cured by talking. People can learn how to cope, but they can't change their biological makeup. So, to tell someone his or her medication is a coward's choice is the same as telling someone who takes medication to stop epileptic fits, or someone with diabetes who takes insulin, or someone who takes medication to thin their blood in order to prevent a heart attack, that his or her medication is the easy way out . . .

It is completely and utterly absurd.

I don't blame Mum for that day in the car park.

At the time, her words yanked roots out of the ground on which I stood. She was the person I trusted most; she was the person whose opinion I held in the highest esteem; she was my mum.

The outburst was cruel and it tore at my already fragile mind, but *she* was not cruel. Mum didn't know; she couldn't understand and that scared the shit out of her.

•

If you're judged for talking about your mental illness, because it is 'showing off', or 'seeking attention', society is essentially insinuating your sickness is *not* something you're meant to talk about. If you feel like you're not meant to talk about it, how can you find your voice in a world where everyone is shouting his or her judgements at you?

A silenced voice is a tragedy . . . and in many ways it's the greatest threat to a person's life.

Silence is the reason people have been able to suffer for years without their loved ones knowing. Silence is the reason people have been able to take their own lives without anyone even realising something was wrong.

Silence is the reason why so many people in the wider community – despite modern medicine, psychiatric and psychological research, studies and breakthroughs – *still* don't understand.

If you talk about it you're just showing off.

Mind over matter . . . you could just be happy if you wanted to.

There is no reason . . . what could you possibly have to be depressed about?

A drug can't fix your problems; pull your socks up!

These are social misconceptions. They are harmful bacteria growing in a Petri dish.

Silence is the warmth and humidity that allows the bacteria to thrive.

Only a voice can exterminate the contents of the Petri dish.

Only a voice can save a life.

16

I Have Faith in Fate

I met a manic South African girl during my first stay in the ICU. Her eyes were the Caribbean Sea, her skin was ground coffee beans, and her hair was a wild mess of brown curls. Dark at the roots, sun-bleached at the ends. Even more notable were her ankles, neck, fingers and wrists – bejewelled with silver bangles from Turkey, beaded strings from India, rose-gold arm bands, and rings with turquoise stones; all of which were stripped from her limbs and taken to the nurses' station the day she was admitted.

Being manic, she had no filter and argued relentlessly with the nurse.

'I'm not even suicidal! I'm not a danger to myself; I want my jewellery! I'm not going to harm myself; I just want it!'

'Regardless of your risk to yourself,' the nurse said, her voice hushed, but stern, 'someone else in this unit may find a piece of your jewellery, or may even steal a piece of your jewellery and –'

'That's ridiculous! Now give me back my jewellery, woman!'

Her smile stretched from ear to ear, where her silver cuff earrings were hidden beneath curls for several hours before the nurse found out. She dressed as if she'd just walked out of an ashram, and she never wore shoes.

I think the greatest gift she gave me was colour.

The day I met her, I'd already spent ten days 'sedated' on the ward. My body was pallid flesh and faint freckles. There's not a lot of sun in between those walls.

This girl was sunlight, she was energy; she was the vibrant burst of paint tubes on my dusty grey canvas.

I told her that my nickname was China and it didn't matter to her that 'Running like China' didn't make sense; she understood. I became her China doll and she loved me, and thought I was brilliant, partly because she was looking through the kaleidoscope of colour that is mania. Partly also because her heart was as stunning as the Red Sea.

She had a plastic ziplock bag filled with crayons, another bag with textas and another bag with pencils. When we parked ourselves on the itchy brown carpet outside the nurses' station, we were allowed to draw in the handmade Indian books her sister had brought in for us. She marvelled at the speed at which I drew and I marvelled at the way colour poured from her fingertips onto the page.

Mania is short-lived. It was her first episode, and while the doctors had tried to warn her, nothing could have truly prepared her for the fall.

I watched the colour drain from her skin; I watched her ocean become murky green water. For the week in which she'd been high, she went back for thirds at breakfast, morning tea, lunch, afternoon tea, dinner *and* supper. *Everything* was delicious; *everything* was divine.

I watched the food lose its flavour on her tongue. I watched the portions on her plate become smaller, until one day she couldn't even bring herself to eat.

She had given me a book with parchment paper, a handpainted cover and a colourful string that you wound around its pages to keep them shut. I loved it because there were no lines. I also had a Spirax exercise book with a glossy yellow cover that I'd used briefly at school, before ripping out the pages with schoolwork and using it as a journal. On days when I wrote, I tried to save my greater ideas and words for the Indian book. Most of what I wrote during those days didn't make sense but I used to read my entries to her. Somehow they made sense to us.

On days when I didn't write, I had a book called *Sophie's World*, which sums up 3000 years of philosophy into one book. I had read it before I had first been put on medication; before my vision became blurry; before the clear waters of my mind clouded and before my hands shook.

Being so heavily sedated meant that the speed at which I read was even slower. The strangest thing was that, while I read painfully slowly, I committed everything to memory. When I read my South African friend pages from *Sophie's World*, it didn't matter that I stumbled tragically over the words because I knew where to find my favourite parts and where to find the greatest philosophical quandaries.

Sometimes she would close her eyes as I read, tilt her head back and lose herself to my voice, while I lost myself to the rhythm of the story.

It was therapeutic for both of us.

Two girls barely there . . . yet barely there *together*.

One afternoon, I was sitting out on the cool aluminium bench, with indigo clouds creeping above, reading a paragraph from *Sophie's World* where the main character learns about the death of Socrates. As my voice was silenced by the final full stop, she sat up straight in her chair and opened her eyes. Tears spilled.

She was a girl raised in a street with grand white houses and trimmed emerald bushes . . . Yet she was also a girl with turquoise nails, a silver nose ring and hair that could never be tamed.

A girl with a different point of view, who looked me in the eye and said, '*You cannot die now.*'

I remember the burn, the tightness; my tears.

'The world needs you. You cannot deprive the world of Sophie Hardcastle. You cannot deprive the world of China Doll . . . Okay? You're not allowed.

'You cannot die now.'

•

Within the walls of the ICU ward, this girl told me stories of distant skies and seas. Her parents were from South Africa, but her Jewish ancestors had walked along the salt shores of the Middle East.

She had been a year above me in school and so while my dreams of year 12 academic success dissolved in that stale air, so did her dreams of travel. She was meant to be on her gap year, she was meant to taste food she'd never tasted before, she was meant to feel the sun on her cheeks and touch a wine glass to her lips. She was meant to walk barefoot through the markets but instead she was there with me.

Cheated.

It wasn't all a waste however; she managed ten days of her trip before her mum flew over to bring her home. I guess if there is a bright side to being manic, it would be how intensely crowded those hours were. She virtually didn't sleep, she ate and relished and yet she lost half her body weight. Strangers became best friends, nights and days blurred together, a wash of pink sunsets and sunrises.

Her words lit up the room as she told me the ten lives she'd lived in ten days.

She'd attended a Jewish high school. 'Everyone goes to Israel after they leave high school,' she told me, 'some even choose not to come back.'

For hours she told me about Shabbat, and her prayers and the way the conservative Kosher families had two sets of kitchenware and appliances so that they could prepare their meat separately from their dairy out of respect for the animal. I listened to the words of her prayers and the names of her holy teachers. I learnt of the atrocities her people had faced. This girl with the ocean in her eyes told me the story of a community so distant, I could not believe that her neighbourhood lay less than half an hour from my own streets.

I asked her if she believed, and she said she thought the core was beautiful, but admitted that having grown up in a glasshouse, it was hard to see through the steam-clouded windows to the outside world.

Then she told me about a boy she knew who had become sick and had turned entirely to Judaism.

Months later, when we were both out of hospital, she told me again about that boy and said that she had tried for a while to do the same. She found great respect for him, but in the end realised that, while her religion would always be a part of her, it would never define her.

Her story led me to consider my own beliefs.

My illness did not turn me to the confines of a religious doctrine. My illness roused faith in something else . . .

Chance. Coincidence.

•

As a child, I attended scripture lessons in primary school once a week, but I didn't understand why my friends and I were sent to different classes. Halfway through I learnt that it was because I was 'Catholic'.

My sister and I had been baptised into the Catholic Church because my mum and her sisters had, after my nan and her sisters had. It was the closest thing we had to a religious lineage.

In my Catholic scripture class, the most memorable story my scripture teacher told was one of a woman who was grieving the loss of her son. She was told to walk into every house in the village and listen to the greatest devastation each person had experienced.

The woman realised that tragedy has no prejudice. Tragedy is chance.

Even more importantly, the woman learnt that there would always be someone licking wounds that were deeper than her own.

When battling a mental illness it is *so* easy to forget the trials and tribulations of others when you are consumed by your own pain and suffering.

For my first four years of high school, I attended a Catholic girls school. My nan and her sisters had sat beneath the same fig tree, sixty years before, when its trunk was thin and its branches were shy. The convent had nuns living in it then, and any girl who set foot on the grounds around the convent had their knuckles smacked with a wooden rod. By the time my sister was in her final year, the school had converted the convent into year 12 common rooms. The girls went across the road in their free periods to swim in the sea, then came back and hung their bikinis on a bronze sculpture of Jesus crucified.

For the few times that I sat in a Catholic church, I appreciated the history. I liked that we were practising traditions that had scarcely changed over hundreds of years. What I didn't appreciate was the religious framework of moral, ethical and spiritual codes that was as cold and stern as the pews we sat on.

As my year 9 maths teacher, with damp salty hair from his morning surf, said:

'I personally don't believe that going to church and singing the hymns makes me a better person. I am good to my wife and set a good example for my children, I live by the sea and I am happy.'

One of the girls in the class interrupted, 'You're not meant to say that, this is a Catholic school.'

He laughed at the irony.

•

I believe in the universe. I believe in nature. I believe in the human being.

I believe in something greater than myself, knowing I will never comprehend its enormity. I believe in the sun, the sky, the mountains, the lakes, the deserts, the rivers, the streams, the stars, the trees . . .

I believe in the wind, the sea and the moon.

I will never fully understand the higher powers of the universe, or the reason for being, and that thrills me.

I am empowered to know that I am here. By chance, we have evolved over millions of years, and I am here today with this body, with this mind, writing this message.

I don't worship a doctrine because I don't believe that I know all the answers.

I believed this when I was young, and, in a way, I forgot it when charcoal clouds rolled over the horizon and made the waves turn green.

Yet those beliefs were part of what brought me back to the surface. Amid the chaos, I realised my faith and I found myself.

•

My skin is pale and painted with freckles and so I have never been one to bake beneath a scorching sun. Instead, I have always found solace beneath the silver splendour of the night.

When I became sick, the moon became my beacon of light. I took comfort in the white orb rising over black glass.

The stars also became a point of reassurance as I reminded myself that they were always there – burning and alive – even if I couldn't see them during the day.

Two years later, when I was well, my friend and I began walking her dog around the headland every day at dusk. It was the beginning of autumn and the air each night became cooler as pale blue skies turned to dark red wine.

One night my friend had to work late and by the time we reached the top of the headland, a full moon was alive on the horizon. My sister, my friend and I walked down through the darkness, and decided we wouldn't take the wooden boardwalk that wound through the trees. Instead, we chose to cut across the golf course.

We were halfway across when we emerged from a cluster of trees onto a green. The manicured grass circle had a diameter of seven or eight metres.

When I returned home that night, I wrote:

On this night, we stumble through a crowd of trees onto a green. Only this green is elevated two or three metres above the surrounding golf course . . . A plateau.

It's like a stage.

The moon is so bright I have a shadow as bold as if it were the middle of the day. I outstretch my arms and sing to the crowd beneath. 'I'M ALIVE!'

It's moments like these that remind me why I was brought back over the fence. It's moments like these that remind me there is always a reason for life.

We dance, us and our brilliant moon shadows, upon the world's stage.

•

The night before the Under 13s branch board event at Nippers it had rained – cool, silent droplets falling on the windowpane. My uncle had died, and as Mum and I had sat on the couch with my dad talking down the phone from the other side of the world, cool, silent droplets were falling on our cheeks.

Mum worried that my uncle's passing would hinder my performance, knowing that I would beat myself up if I didn't meet my high standards. I had come second every year. She told me, like she did before every event, that it didn't matter what place I came, she'd be proud of me anyway.

I told her not to worry, I had Mike on my side now, and watched her manage a smile.

As we broke through the shore waves, there were three of us in the lead – the three girls who were always the top three. Every year it came down to chance, as only a metre or two separated first from third across the line.

This year, however, as the three of us turned the final marker, I felt my board lift on the sapphire sea. I began to glide, moving faster than the other two.

In board races, little waves that do not break but give you a little lift or 'push' are called runners. At first, that's what I thought this was but you can only last on the shoulder of a runner for a few metres at best. Whatever was beneath me was carrying me *much* further.

I looked back – the other two girls were suddenly ten or so metres behind. Stranger still, my arms weren't hurting, my breath wasn't laboured; it was as if someone else was paddling and breathing for me.

I pulled onto a wave and ran up to the finish line a mile ahead of the rest.

When I found Mum after, I told her, 'He was with me.'

She picked me up and squeezed me and with an ecstatic grin she said, 'I'm *so* proud of you.'

I believe in the sun and the sea and the sapphire people who swim beneath the horizon.

·

I was walking along the beach on a break from writing this book when I began thinking about how I used to say prayers as a child. We didn't go to church, so my prayers weren't excerpts from the Bible. I found myself wondering why my prayers had been so important to me.

I think it was the reflection. As a ten-year-old, I would whisper words into my palms, recalling the events of that day, and would then give thanks for everything that had happened to me. I gave thanks for the beautiful things, and

I found ways in which I could still thank the universe for the ugly things. Then at the end, before I kissed my hands and sent my words away on a hot breath of air, I would hope for something in the future.

Gratitude for time passed, and faith in tomorrow: they are two very powerful things. I'd known that when I was ten and lost sight of it as I grew older. On this day, I picked up a dandelion and instead of making a wish, I whispered 'thank you' and sent the seeds away on a hot breath of air. I'd finally re-learnt what was important.

•

When I was a young teen, Dad would take me down to the lookout at Long Reef whenever a southerly screamed beneath grey and green clouds. The wooden platform faced directly south and I would climb up, rugged up in winter jackets, and just stand there, as my hair danced and the wind beat tiny tears from the corners of my eyes.

My lips would curl because nothing compares to that feeling.

I wrote about the wind at school, and when a teacher asked what I thought the wind might say if it could speak, I wrote her a story about a young boy who saw coloured lights in the sea breeze. The soothing voices of the wind told him that they were the souls of those who had lived and the souls of those who were yet to live, swimming effortlessly across peach skies.

As I became sick, I forgot the splendour of 'natural highs'. I forgot the ecstasy of a wind that screams in your face. I forgot how to breathe.

I don't think it was until my fourth admission to a pychiatric hospital, while I was restless with cabin fever, that I remembered the brilliance of wild, stormy weather.

I was given an hour of leave with an accompanying adult and spent the entire afternoon waiting anxiously for a boy with icy blue eyes to finish work and collect me from my room. There was a semi-finished 1000-piece puzzle on the floor and I ran across it when he opened my door, destroying hours of effort in pursuit of an hour of freedom.

He drove me down to the baths at Greenwich, bypassed a fisherman on the commercial dock and parked at the edge of a grassy reserve that led down to a cobbled boat ramp. There were tiny freckles of rain on the windscreen – big enough to see, but not big enough to turn on the wipers.

Outside, the wind tore at my hair as we walked down to sit on the edge of the boat ramp beneath an ashen sky.

'Are you sure you don't want to sit in the van?' he asked. 'It will be warmer.'

'Yes, I'm sure, this is perfect.'

We sat there – my love, the screaming wind and myself – until I had to go back to the hospital.

Sometime later the two of us walked down to sit on chalk sand. I remember how still that day was. The sky and sea were pale and there was not the faintest breeze.

I think it was the first time I had ever told anyone that I believed in the wind. I guess it's not something they teach in the religion syllabus at school.

I told him that it might sound odd, but that the absence or presence of the wind during my life's most profound moments said more about those moments than my words ever could.

The joyous laugh of the sea breeze as my family sailed upwind across a magnificent Fijian sea.

The howl of the starry sky the night a boy unlaced my innocence.

The silent voice of the salty air the day my uncle died.

The grey, windswept ocean that I stood over the night I went to end my life.

As I shared these words with him on that still afternoon, a breath of air rose from the waves, lifting the sand and kissing my cheek.

'See!' I giggled. 'The wind speaks to me.'

He started laughing,

'I like you.'

'And I like you,' he said with a smile.

'What a marvellous coincidence.'

17

Interrupted by Madness

In the semester before I went into hospital for the first time in 2011, we were studying *Waiting for Godot* by Samuel Beckett.

The girls in my class were frustrated because it didn't make sense, yet it made sense to me. At that time, *I* was wandering aimlessly. Time, space and existence were subverted in my own life as I lost my grip on reality. My life had become an absurdist play.

In hospital, my ever-growing obsession with the Surrealist movement of the early twentieth century led me to ask Mum for a copy of the Surrealist Manifesto. When she found that it was not easily accessible, she went to a local second-hand bookshop and found me *Nadja* by André Breton, the founder of the Surrealist movement who wrote the 1924 Surrealist Manifesto.

I am a slow reader, but I read *Nadja* in an afternoon sitting. As in *Godot*, the lack of structure in *Nadja* made sense to me because, at the time, *I* lacked structure.

Breton wrote extensively about a mad, hysterical woman, admiring her for being in touch with her intuition. Her mental illness would strip back the confines of conscious logic to reveal the turbulent waters of the subconscious mind. I remember lying there, psychotic – a mad woman – thinking André Breton would have loved me.

When Mum visited next and I'd told her all the thoughts racing through my mind about Surrealists congregated in Parisian apartments, anteaters on leashes, wine and cigars and chaotic affairs, she'd bitten her lip because she was scared. Nevertheless, Mum and the local second-hand book dealer made calls across Sydney until they finally found *L'Amour Fou* (another work by Breton) in another bookstore. I think the reason Mum was so eager to get it for me was because it distracted me; *anything* was better than leaving me to dwell on my surroundings.

L'Amour Fou, Mad Love.

I became obsessed with the idea that all that is irregular is beautiful. I became obsessed with automatic writing, where the author taps into their chaotic subconscious stream of thought. I guess it's pretty easy to strip away conscious logic when there is none. Many of my journal entries from those early days defy rationality.

I don't really know what it is when the paws tap and the machine purrs, the lime clock comes to life and the wet banana leaves are dripping blood and oh, how badly do I wish to be in between those white concrete walls with grey droplets firing against the red tiles and I curl up beneath white powder, thick and warm and I'm safe. Take me! Take me to where I am home.

I wrote my HSC English major work while I was in hospital and, if anyone read it now, it would be fair for them to assume that I was not thinking 'clearly' at the time.

The story was of two aristocratic teens sent to live among the lower classes with their nanny for protection during the Spanish Civil War as the rebels targeted their elitist family. The girl and boy cousins' world is fractured and distorted like a Cubist painting as bombs disfigure the face of the city and artillery disfigures the faces of the civilians. When their nanny is gunned down, they are ravaged by hunger and turn to each other, satiating their aching bellies with sex. Their wild, devious, glorious intercourse tears at their consciences as they defy their conservative religious bounds.

Starvation and lust become grossly intertwined.

My grandpa showed me the courtesy of reading the story through to the end although I'm sure it would have been a struggle for him. For me however, it was not a story of unorthodox sex, it was a story of a situation that was ugly and messy, that was somehow beautiful.

It was my story.

It was a flash of lightning in a horrendously dark green storm.

It was my *mad* love.

•

I latched onto the notion of 'sweet sour' because it gave me hope.

Being sick made me understand the finality of ash, and the ugliness of the bitter grey. And it made me appreciate the sparks. It made me appreciate the sweet warmth of fire burning, flames dancing, gloriously alive. I latched onto *chance* and *coincidence* because they justified everything that had happened. I came to realise that I had not fallen subject to this illness because I had been an evil child or because I was a bad person. It was by chance, and therefore it was out of my control.

And, as clichéd as this may sound, I am grateful because I wouldn't be writing *Running Like China* had my chemistry been composed correctly. I wouldn't have gained the knowledge and insight that can only be attained through experience . . . I wouldn't have the same capacity to help others. For these reasons, I wouldn't change my situation, no matter how ugly it has been at times.

During a month between hospital admissions, my sister and I watched a British TV series called *Skins*. At that point, I was quite heavily medicated and the episodes blur together when I try to recall them. There is one, however, that resonated with me. It was fuel to my fiery obsession with coincidence.

One character explains to another that there are things in existence that don't obey physical laws. The universe can be erratic and random. That's what makes it marvellous.

I was obsessed with these notions, but I had not truly applied my ideas of *coincidence* to my own situation yet. Not until one October afternoon in 2012.

I'd spent months sailing on smooth seas. That day, however, I found myself on turbulent waters.

I was with a friend painting in a colourful studio wearing paint-stained clothes when the music he was playing suddenly seemed to scratch. I remember the instant devastation and sadness. Paint drained from my body's canvas as if I'd been left out in the rain.

I left my brushes wet and paint tubes open, destroying quality materials, and went to my car. It wasn't until I was driving over the Anzac Bridge that tears arrived.

By the time I reached Neutral Bay, it was nearing two o'clock. The sun was hidden behind a sheet of cloud so fine you could almost see through to the blue sky above. The traffic was okay for Military Road and, as I approached the hill down to the Spit Bridge, driving past a yellow block of flats and a church, it happened.

A kind of 'on your way home from work life-changing epiphany'.

I was gutted and I was angry because for several months I had been stable and had led myself to believe I was 'cured' . . . Like bipolar was something I'd had. Past tense.

I hated how little control I had over it. I hated how unpredictable it was. I hated that, despite doing everything I could to stay healthy, the episodes could and did return.

My friends were making plans. They were travelling, working their way up in their jobs and studying at university – they were working *towards* something. My hands were so tight around the steering wheel my knuckles turned white. I felt I couldn't make plans – that no matter how focused I was, or how hard I worked for my goals, an episode could just kick my feet out from underneath me.

Madness could interrupt my life at any moment.

That's when I passed between the block of flats and the church. That's when I heard my words as if they weren't mine, as if someone else was selling my ideas to me.

All that is irregular is beautiful.

Madness. Chance. Coincidence. Love. Tragedy. Splendour. Heartache. Joy.

The universe is unpredictable, that's what makes this world so remarkable.

For the first time in my life, as I drove that afternoon through faint sunshine, with salty cheeks and my foot on the accelerator, I understood that my illness is unpredictable, and that that doesn't make my life ugly . . .

It makes my life beautiful. It makes my life worth living.

18

Running Like China

In late 2007, a girl with iridescent eyes said I was 'running like China'.

China became my nickname.

'You mean running like a Chinaman?' people would ask.

'No . . . just China.'

I think the name caught on so well because China is not something you can actually run like. It makes no sense; that is why it's brilliant.

In early 2012, after my third hospital admission, I became China. Casting a shadow over my sick self, I had time to heal.

China was more than a nickname, it was a mask I adopted.

I underestimated, however, the fragility of my porcelain skin.

It was only a matter of time before I cracked.

•

After coming home from hospital in February 2012, I started university at Sydney College of the Arts in March. I didn't know anyone and I was as fresh as the modern studios we entered. The scars on my arms had turned white and were invisible at first glance on my porcelain skin. The blood-red scars on my hips were concealed beneath my dress. There were no physical giveaways. For the first time, I had the ability to edit my story, to chop and change paragraphs so that the time Sophie spent in hospital could be obliterated. I was in the process of becoming somebody else, whether I consciously acknowledged it or not.

I was China and no one knew any different.

•

At the time I was struggling to find my feet again socially on the Northern Beaches. Everyone around me had already formed tight-knit cliques while I had been battling my illness. Entering these groups was difficult because I upset the dynamic.

A friend with scarlet lips introduced me to her group of friends as China. They were like a loving family, and if half of them weren't kissing each other, you'd swear they were close enough to be siblings.

Although almost all of them had gone to neighbouring schools to the ones I had, the vast majority of faces were new. It meant that, in the same way I had at uni, I could edit my story.

I was China, and only two or three people knew any different.

This group introduced me to others and I met new faces with blank skin that would later be coloured in with the revealing of vibrant stories. It was tremendously exciting for me in that I knew nothing of them and they knew nothing of me.

China spread like wildfire, and I loved her. I loved her heat; she felt alive.

.

In the beginning, China masked the scars and the prescription pills, the nerves in crowds, the way milky tears welled and my somewhat awkward stance. It allowed me to assume a façade of normality. I wasn't chasing the horizon or trying to cram passionate living into tiny pockets of time the way I had before I got sick. Instead, I was chasing stability.

Maybe I was ashamed; maybe I was trying to sweep the pills and the doctors' appointments beneath the rug like dirt.

Or maybe I was just desperate.

Desperate to paint my skin with the same coloured pigment as the crowd. Desperate to move and dance and laugh and sing the way they all could. Desperate to be in the group . . . safe.

More than anything, I adopted the mask because I so, so badly didn't want to get sick again. And although I wouldn't have admitted it at the time, the new face allowed me to pretend Sophie, the one who was sick, and her dust of cocoa freckles, didn't really exist.

.

When I came home from hospital in February, I had discipline. I had all the pamphlets, all the worksheets and had attended all the therapy sessions to teach me how to best survive outside the walls of the hospital. I knew that I needed to take my medication at the same time every morning and the same time every night. I knew it was advisable to go to bed at the same time every night and wake up at the same time every morning. I knew I needed to stick to my diet so my medications would metabolise effectively. I knew that gradual exposure to social activity was key. I also knew that drugs and alcohol were out of the question.

What I lacked, however, was experience with making it work every day.

As the friends who had met me as China began to outweigh the friends who had known me as Sophie, it became easier and easier to deny the existence of my former self. The dangerous thing, however, was that in denying Sophie, it was really easy to pretend those lifestyle restrictions didn't apply to China.

I began to push the boundaries.

By this point I had been diagnosed with bipolar disorder or temporal lobe epilepsy, which meant I wasn't legally allowed to drive until epilepsy was ruled out. I relied on friends for lifts and would blame them when my parents asked why I had returned home after my curfew.

It's not my fault, he didn't want to leave the party that early and I had to wait for him . . .

In retrospect, I can see how frightening this time must have been for my parents. They still saw their girl who was sick and in need of their loving care and protection. I saw a girl who was eighteen and deserved the same freedoms granted to her peers.

Mum and I argued bitterly.

'Well none of my friends have a curfew!'

'*Sophie . . . None of your friends have spent four out of the last nine months in hospital!*'

The more I marvelled at my porcelain mask, the more convinced I became that Sophie's face no longer lay beneath.

The more I denied my past, the more liberty I demanded in the present.

I started to believe that I no longer needed to act with caution because I was the same as everyone else.

•

I started smoking weed in April 2012. It was only occasional; mostly after dinners that the group would have in a hotel restaurant on the beach central to where everyone lived. Although when you have a mental illness, even smoking weed 'only occasionally' is unforgiving. But the more I split from Sophie subconsciously, the more I believed that China didn't have a mental illness.

In May, I bought tickets for the girl with the golden locks and myself to go to a music festival. We drove up to the rural town in a car convoy of friends. Trailing behind were friends of my new friends who I had never met – new faces with stories yet to be told. I was excited.

We parked and pitched tents on a local sports field. Everyone except me drank there. As we sat, cuddled by the soft morning sun on the tray of someone's ute, I felt nervous. It was one thing to be sober at a party where you arrive at 8 pm and are home by 1 am. It was another thing entirely to know it was 8 am and that I wouldn't be back at the car to sleep until 1 am. Whether I wanted to admit it or not, I was still in the wake of an ordeal and probably didn't have enough energy to actually last the day and night.

It was the first time in my life that I worried I would not be able to keep up. I desperately wanted to move at the same pace as everyone else. So when someone walked out of their tent with a bag of white pressed powder pills, I bought one.

Someone asked, 'If you're not supposed to drink, are you sure you can do that?'

'Yeah, it's fine.'

I spoke those words in an effort to convince myself more than anyone else.

It's fine.

I was arrogant and ignorant; a toxic mix.

With music that rattled my bones, I caught fire.

I laughed harder than I had in a long time.

Flames licked my body and my skin felt hot. I didn't know it at the time, but the heat was creating fissures – tiny cracks in my white porcelain mask.

On the way back to the campsite after the festival, I bought chocolate milk and a meat pie. Wheat- and dairy-free diet slashed. An orange fire blazed and we sat around it on rugs and pillows, wrapped in blankets and woollen clothes. I smoked a joint. Recreational drug-free diet slashed. It was 3 am. Sleeping routines slashed. I forgot to take my purple pills. Medication responsibility ignored.

I was 'on fire'.

I enjoyed that day, regardless of how detrimental it was to my mental health.

It was 12 May and it was significant for two reasons.

The first was that I met the boy with icy blue eyes, the colour of a glacier melting in the spring sun. We had grown up living twenty minutes away from each other. Almost all our friends were mutual, we'd gone to high schools that were within 500 metres of each other and had both been at numerous parties and social gatherings, yet we'd never crossed paths . . . not until that night as we danced on a dirt floor amid a crowd of thousands. White lights cut sporadically through the darkness as our voices were lost to the blare of the music.

When we walked out of the tent after the final song, my ears were ringing and my hand was wrapped in his. We sat beneath the same blanket around the fire, and it was as simple and as innocent as that. Driving home the next day, my friend with the golden locks teased me from the passenger seat. She was sure that I had spent the night with him and I confessed to her that we hadn't even kissed. 'Sure,' she said sarcastically and laughed.

I was driving and absolutely wrecked, focusing my eyes on the distant curves in the highway as I admitted that we honestly hadn't kissed, but that I had this really weird feeling . . . like something big was about to happen . . . something that was greater than myself that I couldn't quite wrap my head around. I had known this boy for less than twenty-four hours and yet I had this bizarre feeling that that wasn't going to be the last I'd see of him.

Months later, I would remind my friend of our conversation that Sunday morning. The two of us would laugh, saying I must be psychic – as if I'd somehow known that the boy with the icy blue irises was about to change everything.

The second reason the day was significant was that I met someone who didn't even know Sophie Hardcastle existed.

I was sitting with the boy with the eyes of a glacier on a picnic rug with someone's quilt wrapped around our tired bodies. Before us, tongues of fire licked dried gum branches.

He was asking for a phone with the internet and/or the Facebook app, but almost everyone's phones were out of battery. Several minutes later, a friend salvaged hers from her bag.

I joked, 'Are you that desperate to update your status?'

He laughed and shook his head.

I watched as he signed in, and typed *China* into the search area. When my profile didn't come up he typed in a different spelling of the name.

'Here,' I said in a hushed voice and took the phone from his hand. 'China is not my real name.'

I typed in 'Sophie Hardcastle', and remember almost feeling embarrassed admitting I was somebody else.

•

By the end of June, I was spending more time at the blue-eyed boy's house, surrounded by trees, than at my own house. He and his parents were calling me Sophie, or Soph, and it felt like a single drop of water landing on the nape of my neck *every* time they said it.

Sophie reminded me of being sick because, apart from my family and lecturers at university, the last time I had really heard it used was when I was in hospital.

I asked him to stop calling me that.

The next day, I walked into the kitchen and his mum turned around, 'Tea, China? I just boiled the kettle.'

Something as simple as a nickname was now a flower with a scent so potent, its fragrance masked any residue of my former self.

China was fun and exciting. She was everything that Sophie wasn't.

But as winter rain dampened the earth, I forgot who Sophie even was.

China slept less, dared more, screamed louder and moved faster. She ate whatever she wanted, she took drugs and she forgot her medication on more than one occasion. But it didn't matter; she could do whatever she wanted, because she was free – she wasn't sick.

Or so I wanted to believe.

The time I truly adopted the porcelain face as my own was when I changed present tense to past tense. For more than two years, I had been living with the mindset, I *am* sick. I *have* bipolar, temporal lobe epilepsy or both.

In July 2012, my mindset shifted, I *was* sick.

I started speaking about bipolar and temporal lobe epilepsy as if they were disorders you can recover from.

With anyone who asked, I spoke of them as if they were disorders I *had* already recovered from.

In many ways, this idea was validated on the second last weekend of July when the boy with glaciers melting in his eyes made me his girlfriend. He'd known snippets of information but it had been that afternoon when I'd taken off the mask and told him Sophie's naked story. I thought he would call it quits after hearing the details. Instead, as he kissed me beneath a streetlight, he said, 'What you told me doesn't change anything about the way I feel about you, because I'm not going out with the person you were then . . . I'm going out with the person you are now.'

I guess ignorance is bliss and bliss was the two of us believing my illness was dead and buried beneath the dirt of my past.

This boy also loved me, China, and no one had ever loved Sophie the way he loved China. In a way, that was another incentive for me to uphold the façade.

In the end, I spent more time at his tree house than I did sitting around my own family's dinner table. In part, the separation was because I had found a *good* love, one where I loved and was loved. I'd found a good love where I was safe.

But admittedly, the separation was partly also because my parents only saw Sophie. They saw a girl who was stable now but who might not be tomorrow. They wanted to look

after me and protect me because they could see my entire
world unravelling all over again if I didn't slow down.

•

Drugs turned Saturday into Sunday without sleep and sapped
the colour out of Monday. The sad thing is that I pretended
I didn't care. I pretended ignoring my family for a whirlwind
of social engagements was okay. I pretended keeping up was
worth the ringing in my ears, the gritty teeth and the stale
breath. I pretended losing my mind on a Saturday night was
worth *losing my mind.*

•

In August I went overseas for two weeks. I walked on black
sand, I surfed and swam in tropical seas and, on the last
night of the trip, I drank two mushroom shakes.

Having already hallucinated while psychotic the year
before, the blend of hallucinogenic mushrooms poured down
my throat really didn't do me any favours. I justified it at
the time, however, because *Sophie* had hallucinated. *Sophie*
had been sick.

I hadn't known psychosis as *China.*

In the final weeks of August, I had two 'episodes' whereby
I experienced intense waves of sadness and felt my skin
shrinking. The first occurred when I was lying in bed in
the early hours of the morning. The room was as dark as

the devastation that washed over me. The boy with ice-blue eyes was woken by my laboured breath and held me.

'A nightmare.'

'Shh . . . you're okay now.' He soothed, cradling me as my tears wet the sheets.

The second occurred when I was walking out of uni one day. My legs became weak and I hid behind a tree for over an hour until it passed.

I pretended the flavour of these episodes was not familiar . . . like they were random, unwarranted spells. I told myself, and I told him, that I couldn't explain why I had just cried so hysterically.

'Just a nightmare,' I lied.

•

In early September I was finally admitted to hospital for a week for epilepsy testing. I had a rainbow stream of wires cascading from my head down to a machine monitor. I had another machine that measured my heart rate and beeped and flashed when the reading fell below fifty. I have a very low resting heart rate and as I was confined to the bed 24/7 (except when going to the bathroom), it beeped and flashed like a stale nightclub, throughout the nights and days.

The tests were seen as inconclusive as I didn't experience one of my 'false memories' or hallucinations while being monitored.

The week was, however, significant for four distinct reasons.

The first was that my mum was beside me in another hospital bed. I was required to have a family member or close friend staying in the room with me at all times so that they could notify a nurse if I had an episode.

It was the most time Mum and I had spent with each other in a long time and, although the circumstances were not ideal, it was *everything* we needed.

That week took me back to being in the car, just Mum and me, driving to surf comps and telling stories of the world for hours on end.

The second significant event was that the boy with the ice-blue eyes came to visit on the first afternoon and stayed while Mum went to her soccer game, passing me from hand to hand as if I were a torch in an Olympic relay.

He helped me carry the cord of wires to the bathroom, joking that I looked like one of the blue people from James Cameron's *Avatar*. He sat with me while I ate my dinner, helping me to navigate my fork through the tangle of colourful vines, and when my mum got back he stayed.

Sitting in a plastic chair beside my bed, this boy told me to close my eyes, saying he'd leave when I fell asleep.

I woke up three hours later to find my hand in his. He was watching the TV and when I told him that he should go, because it wasn't safe to be driving back any later, he managed a weary smile. Then he squeezed my hand, telling me that he didn't want to leave me on my first night, but promised he would soon. 'Just go back to sleep,' he whispered and kissed me on the cheek.

I woke up two and a half hours later to find my hand still in his. The boy with the blue ice in his eyes was asleep in the plastic chair beside me.

Red lights from the monitor lit his body like flashes of pink lightning. I don't think I have been so humbled by anything in my entire life. His love was deep and honest and, in being loved, I was finally able to see my past *bad* loves for what they had truly been . . . ice. They had been ice that was so cold it almost felt hot.

Thirdly, I had time to think . . . to *really* think. In doing so, I started to tap into the desire I had had as a young teenager to change the world.

Reflecting on the night the blue-eyed boy had spent in the plastic chair, I wrote:

They say that the complexity of human emotion is what distinguishes us from animals.

Emotion defines our humanity.

For a long time I sought to be extraordinary, wanting to empower and inspire, wanting to instigate great change.

I remember Mum saying, 'But sometimes it's enough . . . for most people, an ordinary life is enough.'

I remember shaking my head, repulsed by the idea.

I'm not saying now that I'm never going to change the world. Instead, I think that for the first time in my life, I have seen the extraordinary in the ordinary.

I look at my family and marvel at the times all the pieces fall into place at exactly the same moment. And then I look at the times when the family portrait is made up of incongruent sections, where nothing fits together. Yet it's almost as fascinating to see the ways in which they contradict, as it is to watch the way in which they gel together.

And then there was last night . . .

Lying beneath stark white linen with my index finger glowing pink in the dim purple light, and electrodes glued to my scalp.

I open my eyes, moving my body ever so slightly and he wakes.

There are monitors beeping, shoes scuffling, lifts opening and closing and trolleys being wheeled down the corridors, and yet there is a cool silence that envelops us.

He manages a tired little smile and then yawns. Sleepy pink eyelids exaggerate the wild blue of his irises.

It's so calm here, in the eye of the storm. The purple fog wraps around two weary bodies. It's just us.

And I have this, I have this moment and no biological flaw can steal it from me.

To love and be loved; it's a miracle drug – the most extraordinary thing of all.

The fourth significant event was that they took me off my medication for the week so that if the epilepsy was there, they would see it. The problem was that in withdrawing me from my medication, I was exposed once more to the wrath of raw depression.

I fell deep into the abyss, and while it was incredibly dark and dank, I honestly think I needed to experience that fall.

I was beginning to realise my ignorance in assuming that the demons Sophie grappled with were no longer China's concern.

19

A Glacier Melting in His Eyes

In November 2012, I moved into a cottage where a possum
and her two baby possums lived in the roof. The walls
were cracked fibro, the bathroom window was missing two
slats and my bedroom was as wide as my bed. The cottage
was falling apart and yet it was holding me together.

I lived with the boy with the glaciers melting in his eyes
and his best friend, whom I called Panda.

Never in my life have I met two friends as close. Someone
once said of the pair, 'If one falls over a twig, they both fall
over the twig.'

Each consumed copious amounts of ice-cream mixed with smashed Oreos, Nutella, M&M's and lollies. Often they garnished this dessert with Milo and chocolate sauce. Each wore their heart on their sleeve, cared an awful lot for each other and cared an awful lot for me. I was safe.

I learnt a lot from both of them, like how to cook and how to spend way too much time picking the brand of baked beans that will save twenty cents off the final grocery total. I also discovered the joy in bacon and egg fry-ups at 3 am, the hilarity in never leaving a nightclub without being made to leave, the sour taste of off milk and the speed at which a yard of green grass turns to dirt when it becomes a substitute dining room and dance floor.

•

In the months leading up to November, my parents' relationship was disintegrating and that was largely because of me. I had taken them to hell and back and in the process of trying to save me they had lost sight of each other.

My family was screaming as loudly as a great southerly wind, tearing the roof off the house.

A large part of the problem was that I had missed out on a chunk of my teenage years, I hadn't had a normal social life since I was a young sixteen-year-old, and so not only were they trying to prevent me from getting sick again, they were treating me like I was still that age. For me, moving out was an attempt to prove I could achieve independence so that I would be worthy of being treated like an adult. Two weeks after I moved into the cottage, my parents went on the honeymoon they'd never been able to have for their twenty-fifth wedding anniversary. When I picked them up from the airport on their return, their skin was sun-kissed and glowing. Each had found their best friend again.

.

On our first night at the cottage, we heated up bolognaise mince that Panda's mum had made us, and stirred it in the saucepan with a metal ruler from my pencil case. Outside, we were welcomed to the neighbourhood with a display of fireworks that just so happened to be shooting over Long Reef golf course for a wedding.

On our first weekend living at the cottage, I took a capsule.

Everyone else witnessed the magical glory of a blue moon.

I witnessed hallucinations, terrifying beyond belief.

I was acutely suicidal, screaming into the shadows at 4 am. I could see the house burning when I opened my eyes *and* when I closed them. It was like being in pitch-black darkness where you can't even tell if your eyes are open or shut. The boy with the blue eyes put me in the shower and I screamed as I saw cuts all over my naked body. My blood was streaming over the tiles and circling around the drain. 'There's nothing there,' he assured me, running his hands over my skin, 'see . . . nothing . . . You're okay, it will pass.'

For the next six weeks, I was clean.

My cheeks bloomed like cherry blossoms and the whites of my eyes were as clear as spring water. More wonderful than any physical differences, however, was the way in which my mind came alive. Within two weeks, my inner voice spoke with remarkable clarity. I was able to process thoughts much more easily and could converse more freely.

Being articulate was worth missing out on a Saturday night chemical kick.

It wasn't really until mid-December that fissures in my porcelain skin began to show again. Like it had the year before, 20 December shook my bones.

I was China, but my birthday was the realisation of another year; it was a stark reminder of my former self.

I mentioned the random quaking of my limbs, the sudden lump in my throat and the glassing of my eyes to my psychiatrist and he added an anti-depressant to my medication. A very low dose of a small white pill to help support my mood stabiliser.

I felt great within three days and reminded myself that those depressive episodes didn't happen to *me* anymore.

Eight days later, the boy with the icy blue eyes had packed a bed, dress-ups, alcohol, straw hats, sombreros, body paint and a bag of summer clothes into his blue and white van. We were going to a music festival.

At the bottom of a lush valley, we camped beside a shady creek that we dived into to escape the dry tongue of summer.

Inside the festival, colour and energy exploded like succulent berries bursting with juices.

Beneath the circus tent, music made bones shake and chapped lips curve in rapture. Dirt was kicked up from the floor; we danced amid clouds of orange dust.

The valley was alive, and yet I was so alone.

The festival went for four days and, as strange as it sounds, I had no one to talk to. *Everyone* was on another level from me. Their minds were racing, their mouths were racing, their limbs were racing and I was sober. Some were hallucinating, other friends were so bent they didn't recognise me; and a few were so stoned they had melted back into the earth. It was quite possibly the strangest social environment I had ever been in; friends surrounded me and yet I could not have felt more alone. In a way, it reminded me of being depressed or manic, where I want nothing more than to move in sync with the rest of the world. By the third day, all I wanted to do was travel at the same pace. I wanted to run with them.

I smoked so much weed my eyes were juicy beetroots, and that night I swallowed pills and a capsule.

I was out of my mind and yet I was the furthest thing from happy. It was like being trapped in one of those dreams where no matter how hard you try, you just can't find that person you're looking for.

I spent the first day of 2013 with a cracking headache and a body sticky with sweat, salvaging our belongings from a campsite littered with egg cartons, beer cans and torn streamers. By the late afternoon, we'd made it onto the highway and were driving home in silence.

At the cottage, there were two windows in the lounge room that faced a brick wall outside, and a door that led into the kitchen. That room was dark all day, all night, all year round.

I spent the first three weeks of 2013 sliding between the murky green shadows in that room, watching episodes of *Breaking Bad* on a TV that was almost as big as the wall. Sodden tea bags hung under my eyes and my lips were pale and blistered.

.

We were meant to go to Thailand, the blue-eyed boy and me. He paid for the accommodation, but the trip was sacked when we couldn't afford to actually get there.

Instead, in the fourth week of January, he piled our belongings into the blue and white van and we left. We were going to Kangaroo Island in South Australia, with no idea how we were going to get there, or when we would even arrive. Just south of Sydney, we turned onto a scenic route and he laughed, 'Highways are for when you're going somewhere, and we're not going anywhere!'

In hindsight, it was just as much a trip to try and catch my fall as it was an adventure.

Every time I stuck my head out the window in amazement, or gasped and pointed at something remarkable, or smiled for so long that it burnt my cheeks he told me, 'Hold on to that.' The boy with the blue ice eyes would tell me to write that moment down so that if we got home from our trip and the dark hands wrapped around my skull, I'd be able to read the journal entries and remember how good those moments had felt.

We had $900 and we spent at least $650 on fuel on our 4000 kilometre journey. The remaining money was spent on tins of tuna, Corn Thins, herbal tea, curry paste from a rural market, fruit, lentils and clothes from an op shop. We also bought a trinket from every place we stopped and superglued it to the dashboard. Eating at a diner or pub quickly became a luxury.

The adventure was a breath of ocean air, and I loved it because it was raw. The cold salty winds bit our skin, the ocean spat foam high into the sky, the clouds were ashen, the bush was dry, the earth was red and the road seemed endless. I loved it because I discovered that *real* love is raw love.

The only problem was that I thought a love that was real would stop me from falling back into the abyss. I thought it meant I was safe, that he could make porcelain unbreakable.

·

For the first few days back home, I moved as if I was sleepwalking.

On the Thursday, I saw my psychiatrist with the snow beard and he ruled that the small white tablet had actually made me manic. An anti-depressant doesn't make you feel great within three days. Even though it had been a low dose to support my mood stabiliser, it had swung me up. I'd been high and the drugs I'd taken on New Year's Eve had been the perfect trigger for my downfall. In an effort to salvage the situation, he took me off the white medication. In the weeks that followed, I experienced the most intense rapid cycling I'd ever encountered.

I was morbidly depressed and learnt what it is to love someone when you can't *feel* love.

Depression takes away your libido and your affection – a lifeless heart in a cage of dry bone ribs.

I know that I love him, but some days my blood runs cold and I forget how that love feels. He kisses me and I don't taste it.

He tells me I am his sunshine, but what if this star has already exploded? What if I am a black hole lost in space?

To the boy with the icy blue eyes, thank you for waiting for me.

For two days after my time in the black hole, a fire burned inside me, making my porcelain skin expand; more pieces cracked from my cheeks.

I spoke louder, faster and made less sense. I was like a painter who didn't know when to put down her brush. The artwork was a masterpiece, and yet I kept painting. I kept painting until I'd ruined it.

I tried to put my hand down his pants while we were grocery shopping, again and again until he was red in the face with embarrassment.

To the boy with the icy blue eyes, thank you for making me tea. Thank you for holding me until I was still.

In the days that followed, I fell.

For the first time, China was well and truly suicidal.

By Tuesday, I couldn't get out of bed. He lay in his work clothes with me. I burst into tears and told him I was sorry, but that I didn't see a future. His response was remarkable.

'If one day you do forget and you stop fighting . . . if you can't see yourself walking around tomorrow, I will see you. I will always see you in the future and I'll fight every day to make sure you're still here when I wake up tomorrow.'

To the boy with the icy blue eyes, thank you for fighting for me.

The following day, I cracked open the porcelain with a blade.

My mum found me; she was heartbroken but she wasn't angry. I think that was the difference this time – she understood, and although it was still incredibly confronting, she knew that it was no one's fault. She knew my skin was shrinking for reasons no one could really explain. But more than anything, Mum knew I was in a place where I was so desperate to get out, I would resort to my own means of alleviation.

My heart ached for her as she held back the tears. Unlike the other times I had been found, however, her level of understanding soothed the hysteria. She silenced my cries, 'Shh, it's going to be okay, baby, and I'm taking you to get fixed up.' Her words were a soft blanket, straight out of the dryer. *Warm.*

Mum dropped me at Dad's work. His office was the calm in the eye of the storm and I spent the day there, sleeping beneath his desk. When Dad dropped me back to the cottage that night, the boy saw my bandaged limb and his heart bled.

To the boy with the icy blue eyes, thank you for loving me when I no longer loved myself.

The next day, I was 'fine'.

I was lively and excited and energetic, and completely in denial of the mess I'd made of my flesh the morning before. I travelled with the blue-eyed boy to his work, before taking the blue and white van to my work. Pink tears glassed his eyes as he got out, and begged me, 'Please, please, please, be careful.'

I remember bouncing in my seat telling him, 'I'm fine! I'm fine!'

'Please be careful,' he said once more before disappearing into his work building.

The drive to my work was about ten minutes, but it took me almost half an hour. The first sign that I was losing my sense of reality occurred 500 metres up the road from his work building when I passed an Indian girl in her school uniform walking with her head down. I saw her entire life story in a matter of seconds as if it was a motion picture. I saw her finding a boy in two years when she was seventeen who would love her like nothing else and I wanted to pull over the van to tell her to have hope . . . *Believe me! He's coming; I've seen it!*

Thankfully, I still had enough sense to continue driving and not harass the schoolgirl.

Further down the road, I drove past an RSL club where there was a group of elderly people out the front waiting to get on a bus. I burst into laughter, literally choking on my own breath. I was hysterical and I made an illegal U-turn at a busy intersection before driving back, desperate to take a photo of the group. It was the funniest thing I had ever seen and yet there was *nothing* to be amused by.

Hanging out the window with my iPhone, I took several blurry snaps before the sound of a car horn directed my attention back to the steering wheel and I realised I was driving on the wrong side of the road entirely. I swerved back into my lane, and while you would expect the fright of the near head-on collision to provoke some level of rationality, I only laughed harder.

By the time I got to work, hot tears were pouring like a dark summer storm. My sides were splitting, my lips were ripped and my cheeks were burning from laughing so hysterically.

My boss thought I'd taken acid as I tried to explain the hilarity of my recent encounter with the group of old people, although very few words fell from my tongue with any logical order. He told me to sit down and have something to drink, unsure whether to be amused or frightened by my absurd state.

I sat on the floor, sculled a huge glass of water and wrote a text message that I sent to Mum and the blue-eyed boy. I started with '0900 hours, China's weather report . . .' before rambling for three pages. All the while, my body shook in this state of ridiculous hilarity.

Mere minutes after I pressed send my mum rang. My dad was on his way to come and get me.

In many ways, manic days are just as devastating as nights spent in the abyss.

My dad was heartbroken when he picked me up that morning. I had energy, I had life, but I was far from being his little girl.

I guess for me, mania is singing karaoke, badly.

Everyone's ears are hurting, and they're begging you to stop, but you just keep belting out that chorus because you're convinced you sound like Beyoncé.

•

The Thursday I spent laughing at a group of retirees was 14 February 2013. It was the first Valentine's Day I had spent with the boy with the icy blue eyes.

It was the first Valentine's Day I had spent with anyone.

I believed a boy with a glacier melting in his eyes could stop the sun sliding behind pink clouds and disappearing behind the mountains.

I was ignorant in believing real love would stop me from relapsing.

The truth is, love cannot stop daylight from melting in the late afternoon. It cannot bear down on the horizon to prevent the silver moon from rising.

Love cannot stop darkness from saturating the sky.

Instead, love simply meant that there was someone to hold my hand until dawn.

•

I was admitted to hospital for the fifth time, carrying a single blood-red rose, and a pocket full of porcelain pieces.

China was in pieces.

20

Second Chance

I had been so convinced I was healthy and stable, and that
my episodes of psychological anguish were a thing of the
past, that finding myself on a pysch ward, more than a year
after my last admission, absolutely annihilated me.

I was devastated and yet those three weeks would end
up being the most beneficial three weeks I had ever spent
in a psychiatric institution. My porcelain skin was shattered
and beneath it I stood naked and unbound. There was no
room for pretending.

I'd been treated for bipolar for several months by this
point but it was during this admission that the diagnosis was

formally made. It woke me to the reality of the disorder. It also allowed me to fully understand the way in which my loved ones missed me.

That admission was well and truly my second chance.

•

For the first four days, I left my room only to eat and go to the bathroom. I was either sleeping twelve hours, or barely sleeping at all, staying up well after midnight drawing with coloured crayons and chalk.

I refused to take the sedative cocktail I had taken in the past and so nothing was numbed. My emotions were raw and I missed the boy with the icy blue eyes. And he missed me, sleeping on my side of the bed at home.

On my first night in hospital, he sent me a text reminding me that I was his sunshine. He visited me every chance he could. I was torn because I knew he was hard-pressed with work and TAFE, and that the hospital was far away. He was going out on a limb for me and I worried that the branch would break and that he would fall.

At the same time, however, I wanted him there, and I wanted my mum and my dad and my sister there because I was hurting and they were the soothing touch of a hand, gently wiping away the tears.

I felt guilty and I didn't really know how to deal with it.

I attended a youth group in the hospital. For the last fifteen minutes we were given the chance to ask the psychologist whatever question we liked.

I asked what you're meant to do when you feel bad for someone at home – when you feel bad for putting him or her through all of this.

She replied that it was a common question, and that a lot of people experience this feeling of guilt. Her tone was even and her words were clear and concise as she continued, 'Ask yourself: would you do the same for them? If the roles were reversed and they were in hospital, would you do the same for them?'

I nodded, 'Yes, absolutely.'

She smiled. 'Well, all you can do then is make sure they know. Make sure they know how grateful you are.'

The next day, I made cards for my family, and made a video on my laptop of all the pictures of the boy with the icy blue eyes and me. When I showed it to him after two days of editing, he was a little taken aback by how neurotically I had worked on the film. Nevertheless, I said 'thank you', realising how important it is to remind those extraordinary people how grateful I am.

·

After the initial shock had passed, I was angry. I was pissed off that after a year and a half, after everything I had achieved at uni and in building my social life back up, I was in hospital *again*. I was devastated that the boy with the icy blue eyes had seen *Sophie* return, and I was devastated that something I thought I had recovered from was a reality again.

In my second session as an in-patient with my psychologist, we were sitting in a room with no windows, with air that made my tongue turn to dust in my mouth. I didn't need to tell her I was pissed off; she could see the dark cloud hanging over my head.

'You will relapse,' she told me. 'You will probably relapse multiple times, but each time you relapse you will get better at dealing with it and your episodes will become less severe.'

I zoned out. I didn't like the way she was painting my future. I was still in denial.

During our next session, we sat again in the room with no windows.

This time when she said, 'Sophie, you need to accept that you probably *will* relapse again, it's part of your disorder,' I swallowed the words, rather than spitting them straight out onto my lap.

But I didn't like the way they sat in my stomach and so I zoned out again.

Finally, in our fourth session, I'd had a few days to digest her words.

She told me, 'You need to accept it, because the more upset and annoyed you get every time your episodes return, the longer they will take to pass. You need to accept that you will have times in your life when they do come back, and if you simply get angry at the fact that you're feeling like this again, it's going to make it worse.'

My favourite philosopher, Socrates, said true insight could only come from within and, no matter how many times you try to teach someone something, they will never fully appreciate the lesson until they have understood it for themselves.

It was a Wednesday, sitting in that stale room with no windows, when her words finally clicked. It was as if I'd been trying to build a house with my bare hands and someone had just arrived with tools.

After the session, I wrote in my journal:

I've found my weakness . . . Acceptance.

I know this storm is going to pass. My problem is that I cuss and spit at the dark clouds, pissed off that they've even rolled in − pissed off that they've spoilt my day.

What I'm beginning to understand is this . . .

What point is there in resenting the weather?

The punches I throw will not lessen the drum of the rain as it beats against my body . . . They will only tire my arms.

My cussing and foul swearing will not keep my clothes dry . . . Such screams will only scratch my throat.

For beneath the downpour, my shirt sticks to my bust, and my sopping wet hair sticks to my face.

There is nothing I can do. I cannot control bad weather, but I can learn to accept it.

I can accept my place beneath the downpour and can learn to dance in the rain.

•

Towards the end of the second week of my hospital admission, two girls as sweet as honeycomb visited me. I was granted leave and they took me to dinner at a Thai restaurant. I remember the dark wooden tables, lime-green walls and blood-orange napkins, and that they bought me a bowl of green chicken curry, which left hospital food for dead.

One girl has almond eyes and slender hands; the other has creamy caramel skin and remains one of the kindest people I have ever known. I only had an hour and a half's leave and, while my movements were slow, my tongue hesitant, my skin shrinking and my heart aching, those two girls dragged light into that dim pocket of time.

Returning to the hospital, they said goodbye with kisses and hugs, and handed me a brown paper bag. When they had left, I opened the bag and pulled out a dream catcher the one with the slender hands had crafted. It was the colour of a burnt sunset with a clear stone in the centre to ward off negative energy and a seashell dangling from its base to remind me of home. Each manic night after their visit, I put away my crayons and closed my eyes, holding my dream catcher above my face, allowing the pale feather to kiss my eyelids as one hour melted into the next.

And it was in those smooth hours that my skin began to heal and I came to consider the cruel obsession that is self-harm.

For over two years, my illness had clouded the waters of my mind and impaired my judgement.

I had clung to my means of relief because it was an oasis in a desert . . . when in reality, my oasis had only ever been a mirage.

In realising this, I found my way out of the desert and haven't torn my skin since. I haven't even looked back.

I also started reading Khalil Gibran's *The Prophet* again.

One quote stood out for me when I read it the first time in 2012, although it was not until the second read in 2013 that I really latched on to its words.

You shall be free indeed when your days are not without a care, nor your nights without a want and a grief. But rather when these things girdle your life and yet you rise above them naked and unbound.

I had been dwelling on the fact that I was nineteen with bipolar disorder, in hospital, on a strict diet, and even though I had refused the sedative, my psychiatrist had added a second mood stabiliser to my cocktail. I had been dwelling on the idea that 'everyone else' was partying and travelling and bathing in a February sea, eating whatever they pleased and sipping on *real* delicious cocktails.

I guess that's why Gibran's idea resonated with me.

I wrote in my journal:

Today I have realised that what's upsetting me the most is the lack of control I have in making choices – my lack of freedom.

I look at all my friends deciding to go travelling. They put plans in place, they save up and they go. I look at those deciding to go to uni; they choose a course and they work towards completing their degree and entering the workforce.

And then I see myself and I'm in hospital.

And I'm about to miss my first week of uni.

And I've gained a little weight.

And I'm not responding as well as I should have in these two weeks.

And so I cry dirty tears into his lap.

What I don't see is this . . .

I am overcoming adversity.

I am writing despite the ashen fog that clouds my mind.

I am reading a book, despite my weary, sticky eyelids, and despite the pain that pinches the back of my eyeballs when I glance at a light.

I love despite the way depression numbs my lips, silences my heart and drains warmth from my fingertips.

I AM WRITING, I AM READING, I AM LOVING IN SPITE OF THIS ILLNESS.

This empowers me.

This makes me proud.

I can no longer focus on what aspects of my life are hindered by bipolar.

I can no longer focus on what bipolar takes from me.

Instead I can focus on the achievements I make in spite
of bipolar.

That is how I am free.

•

I started attending a group called 'mindfulness'. The group
room had a huge, unbreakable window and when the afternoon sunshine poured through it was like hot light heating
up water in a fish bowl.

On this morning, however, the sky was overcast and the
room temperature was tolerable. I took a seat in the corner
as the psychologist entered and gave a brief outline as to
what mindfulness is.

Essentially mindfulness is about centring yourself in the
present. It is about neither dwelling on the past, nor worrying
about the future, but simply confining your thoughts to your
immediate existence. The psychologist described our minds
as being the pendulums of old grandfather clocks, constantly
swinging between the past and the future. Mindfulness aims
to disable the pendulum so that it hangs still in the middle.

The psychologist then encouraged us to close our eyes
and relax . . .

'Draw back to the anchor of your breath.'

After the session, I wrote this in a journal:

*It's about this moment, living now, in this instant . . . It is
about tasting the flavour on your tongue right now. It's about
the curve of your spine, the temperature beneath your skin, the*

filling of your lungs and the movement of your rib cage. It's about the sweat that lines the contours of your palms.

I don't think I'm meant to feel alive, or invigorated . . .

No.

I think it just provides a few moments of rest. It's a few moments where I am neither behind nor ahead, I am simply here.

•

I had worn my porcelain mask for a year. I'd become cocky.

I abused the measures that had been put in place to maintain my mental health, and my porcelain skin had cracked.

Bipolar had been a dormant volcano that I'd assumed to be extinct. Inevitably, it exploded and my mind blew all over the walls.

The aftermath saw me covered in the ash of depression.

From the black earth, however, I found my second chance.

I stopped dwelling on circumstances that I could not control. Instead, I did everything that I *could* do to help myself. I attended groups, I started to pay attention in my one-on-one sessions, I read the handouts and I started writing this book.

With my second chance, I learnt to control what was in my power, and to accept what wasn't, and although I would not wish my experiences on anyone, I am grateful for the clarity of my nineteen-year-old voice.

Did you know *Sophie* means wisdom?

When I went home, I was still China . . . but I carried Sophie's wisdom.

I went to bed and woke up at the same time. I took my meds at the same time each day and each night. I ate well, according to my diet, and I refused the temptations of drugs or alcohol.

Two or three weeks later, we found a rat in our cottage kitchen. The boys chased it around the house, while I screamed and jumped onto the couch. For the first time in two and a half years, I was scared of something.

21

Family

Quite possibly the most difficult words to write in this book have been the words wrapped around my family.

A mental illness often makes your attention turn inwards. I became oblivious to my family's suffering.

In writing this book, I have had to recall details from a time when I was numb and insensible through the lens of someone who is now sane and able to fully comprehend the severity and implications of certain actions.

I have realised their anguish, and in doing so, I am riddled with guilt.

·

During my first two-month stint in hospital, my then fifteen-year-old sister wrote a message on my laptop. It read:

You would think that it would be easier as time goes by, but honestly I miss you more and more every day.

I remember seeing the note and reading the words, but I was numb. I didn't feel the weight of them.

I didn't realise how many times she would have walked into my room at home while I was in hospital, out of habit, to tell me a joke or ask me a question, or even just to sit on my bed and chat. I didn't consider the way her limbs would turn stiff or the way her eyes would glass as her mind caught up with the facts. I wasn't there; she was alone.

I didn't realise how painfully her school classes dragged on. Or how she didn't hear much of what her teacher said because she was thinking of her big sister sitting in a room where the windows were sealed shut.

I didn't think about how deathly silent the dinner table was while I was in hospital.

I didn't understand how it felt for my family to drive for an hour, climb a staircase, press a button, wait for the nurse to buzz them into the ICU, and then wait for the nurse to take them in pairs to my room only to find that I'd had a bad day.

They would be unable to reason with me, unable to have a real conversation with me.

And I am *so* sorry that I did that to them . . . that I did not realise their anguish.

I am so sorry to my dad, whose tender touch was not enough to prevent this.

I am so sorry to my sister, my silent warrior.

And I am so sorry to my mum, who stood to fight with an aching heart – who lost her job because she chose her daughter over turning up to meetings on time.

She was the one who visited me twice a day, no matter what state I was in, or how many times I told her to leave.

She was the woman who would never let me forget I had a family to come home to.

What I have recently come to understand, however, is that if I were to dwell only on the ways in which they suffered, guilt would turn me sour.

I told Mum how I felt and she shook her head and said, 'You can't feel guilty, it was not your fault.'

She was right because there *is* an imbalance inside me, a biological defect. There *is* a hand that grabs my head and drives its fingernails into my skull, a hand that I do not control.

I have come to realise that I cannot promise my family *I will never get sick again . . . you will never relive the ordeal.*

So that is why I commit myself to every little factor I *can* control. Rather than dwelling on the guilt, I channel it, committing myself to a lifestyle that gives me every fighting chance to ward off a relapse.

In maintaining my mental health, I am preventing my family from reliving such excruciating events. That is the way I show them I am sorry – by doing all I can to manage this disease.

•

People fear the unknown, and in the beginning, I had no idea what was going on with me, so I couldn't lessen my family's fear.

My mum was hot with anger when I was first admitted, but being the strong-minded woman that she is, she set a great example for my dad, sister and her friends by asking 'Why?' She hassled the doctors for answers, read the brochures, bought the books, and followed the links to the websites. Filling herself with knowledge, she was eventually able to empathise with me. It helped save my life.

•

When I relapsed in early 2013, the boy with the blue ice in his eyes said, 'I want to help you so badly, I want to fix this so badly. But there is only so much I can do when you sabotage my efforts by not helping yourself. Please, *please* let me help you by starting to help yourself.'

At the time I was in hospital and I missed him and my family, and my little white cottage, in a way I had never missed anything. I learnt from another patient's story, however, that if I were to go home too early, it would devastate everyone who loved me. I would be able to sit in my lounge room and sleep with him in my own bed, but the blue-eyed boy and my family would not see *me*. They would see a girl still gripped by an ugly illness despite weeks apart.

The boy with blue ice in his eyes was there to support me, as was my sister, Mum and Dad, but if I wanted to make it home to them, I needed to take responsibility for my condition.

Despite being confined within the walls of a hospital, I harnessed all the energy I had. I went to groups, saw my doctors, took my medication and asked for the help of nurses when I needed it. The more time and energy I deposited in each session, the more I benefited my health.

A nurse's soothing hand on my back at 1 am may not have compared to the warmth and safety of Mum's hug, but it was my best shot at making it home. I was so determined to be back with my loved ones that I seized every opportunity to strengthen my body and mind. I was granted leave and would plead with anyone from home to drive over so that they could take me out on a walk.

Even at my weakest points, when dark clouds hovered in hospital corridors, I sought to do at least one small thing each day to improve my health, realising that anything I did to help myself, was helping my loved ones waiting at home. For example, on mornings that were so bleak I didn't think I could move I rewarded myself with watermelon for getting out of bed and into the shower. No matter how small, one act is better than none.

I missed my family, and they missed me, so I fought for a better me.

•

Two visits from members of my extended family taught me meaningful lessons.

The first was when my nan saw me in the ICU. I was bandaged up and she asked, hesitantly, what had happened. I told her I had hurt my arm and she smiled and said, 'Oh well, I hope it heals okay' as if I was a little girl and had fallen over in her backyard . . . as if it was an accident that she could tend to with a grandmother's softly spoken words.

The encounter taught me that, for some loved ones, certain details will always be a little too tender and that I needed to respect that.

The second was when my uncle visited me in the ICU. He is the younger brother to my mum and her two sisters; he's the golden child. He is the most charismatic, articulate person I have ever met. Yet, unlike almost every other person who visited, he didn't tell me what to do. He didn't give me a big spiel about how much everyone loved me and he didn't pour life advice onto the carpet. Instead, he just sat, while I ate lunch on my bed, and listened to the illogical things I was saying.

A year later, he *showed* me his life advice when he was in a motorbike accident that left him in hospital for six months. The doctors told him he would never be able to talk again, let alone move the right side of his body.

Last week we had lunch. He was asking me about my latest book, while eating dumplings with chopsticks held in his right hand.

He taught me that the best advice of all is not spoken.

•

Ambrose Redmoon said, 'Courage is not the absence of fear, but rather the judgement that something else is more important than fear.'

My mum is courageous.

My dad is courageous.

My sister is courageous.

They knew I was lying on the seabed with indigo lips and a cold, silent heart. It was dark down there and I was still. They know how terrifyingly deep the ocean is, and what creatures lie beneath. And despite being riddled with fear, they decided something was more important and chose to dive down in spite of their trepidation.

They chose to bring me back from the dead.

22

Change

'The only constant is change.'

I was thirteen when I read that line on a boy's t-shirt. I was sitting beneath a great pine in my wetsuit with sand stuck to my scalp and the tips of my hair crystallised with salt. The quote was written in bold letters on yellow fabric. I remember it vividly because I was looking at it for a long time; my stare lingering even after the boy noticed me.

I was meant to be studying the surf, preparing for my next heat in a junior comp, but all I could think about was the quote. I guess it was the first time I had truly considered change.

The only thing you can count on is change. The only certainty in our lives is that our lives are uncertain, unpredictable and unstable.

Everything fluctuates.

This revelation was daunting. It is important to remember, however, that just as your life can be flipped upside down in an instant, it can also be flipped back.

So just as my life had changed tragically when I sank beneath the surface, it changed magnificently when I rose to breathe once more.

•

I had started my Visual Arts degree at Sydney College of the Arts (SCA) after finishing school because it was structure. It was routine bus trips and scheduled classes. And there were trees, so many magnificent trees, and an emerald carpet of grass that stretched down to Sydney's stunning harbour.

The college's location was a mental asylum . . . *was* a mental asylum from the early 1800s until the mid-1900s. Old sandstone buildings had been converted into studios for the modern *mad* artist.

I first heard about the degree when talking to a girl in the outdoor area of the hospital during my second admission. Her eating disorder was eating her. It had chewed her body down to the bone, but I didn't look at the hollows beneath her cheeks. Instead, I was lost in her dark eyes. She had a dream catcher on her forearm and we shared the same name.

If she were a flower, she would be a sunflower.

This girl had told me about SCA. She was enrolled there but had taken some time off to heal.

I remember feeling excited about it, which was a big deal. I told Mum and she was excited because I was excited.

We went to the open day the following week. I got special leave for four hours. There was light in Mum's eyes.

As we drove in, I was sold on the trees. I said, 'Yep, this is it,' and Mum was ecstatic. It wasn't until we were walking through the buildings that she enlightened me to the history of the place. 'Are you serious? I'm on leave from a psychiatric hospital, why would you tell me that now?'

We laughed.

A month later I returned with Mum for an information day when artists, tutors, supervisors and lecturers sat individually with applicants and advised them on how to best prepare their portfolios for the interviews that would be taking place a few weeks later. It was in a big hollow hall with tables around the perimeter, dark walls and hardwood floors. Along one wall was a row of chairs that students sat in waiting to be called. Everyone had canvases and portfolios and sketchbooks to show the advisors. Very few had their mums.

Never in my life had I felt so self-conscious about my body. I'd always been extremely athletic but having put on so much weight in hospital, I remember thinking *everyone* was staring at my bloated stomach and chubby limbs while we waited. At that point, I was also still on the drug that gave me hot flushes. I held Mum's arm as my face, neck and chest burnt crimson. My hands shook from the lithium. And as the international artist Lindy Lee began asking me about my work, the cocktail of drugs wiped my memory and my lights turned off. Then I felt the heat climb up the back of my neck, over my scalp and wash down over my face yet again. Mum squeezed the hand of her little tomato.

'It's okay to be nervous,' Lindy Lee told me, 'take your time.'

Yeah . . . *Nervous.*

I came around after a minute of silence and, although my fingers were still shaking, I took her through my process diary. 'I love this,' she said brushing her fingertips over a newspaper article on the Australian artist Euan MacLeod that had been glued across two pages of my process diary. 'You've captured a moment in time.'

Her smile was sincere, but temporary, so I pushed on, explaining my work in as much detail as I could – which sounded ridiculously vague compared to my usual healthy, articulate voice.

When I was done, the silence was momentary.

'When you're not painting, what do you like to do?'

I was honest. 'I love to paint, I also surf, I love the ocean, but I *really* love to write.'

I watched her lean back in her chair. The corners of her mouth curled upward and it was as if her eyes had changed the slightest shade in colour.

'And what do you love to write?'

I told her about my most recent work, the story of the two aristocratic cousins in the Spanish Civil War. I told her how their world is fractured, and they're starving and that they appease their appetites with intimacy. I probably would have stopped there, had I been in a fit psychological state, but instead I continued; I told her how they 'dance in the inferno', and how flames lick their naked, dangerously intertwined bodies as they're consumed by lust. Their relationship is unorthodox, chaotic and convulsive. But it is beautiful. It's their salvation.

In hindsight, my neurotic obsession with the fragile relationship between beauty and chaos had well and truly stemmed from the soil of my mental illness. But it was how I made sense of the mess. It was how I learnt to see tiny embers alight in a pit of ash.

I remember how my face flushed yet again with red ink.

'Just one minute,' she said, standing and walking to the front of the hall where a small information desk stood.

'You okay?' Mum squeezed my hand. 'You're going good, it's tough, but you're doing really well.'

Lindy Lee returned a minute later with a yellow form.

'We don't normally do this but I would like to fast-track you into the course. You don't have to go to the interview. You're in.'

When Mum and I walked out of the hall into the sun-drenched courtyard Mum held up the yellow paper and yelled, 'Yeah! How good's that!'

It was so beautiful, it was the happiest I'd seen her in months.

On the way home, we got hot chocolate to celebrate, and then for weeks after, she told every friend who rang the house.

·

It was structure. It was safe. It was something to do and it allowed Mum to work again. It gave her time off from being a carer. It gave her freedom.

University also gave me a small handful of characters who would forge new, exciting pages in my story after many chapters filled with bleak words and bland imagery.

The most colourful was a boy who burst the safety bubble I'd been floating around in for months. Never before had I seen a boy with so little body fat consume so much sugar. The first afternoon we went back to his house he dipped Belgian chocolate coins in peanut butter until the tub and bag were finished. A great bowl of Froot Loops, Coco Pops, Cheerios, Frosties and Weet-Bix ensued at 4 pm. He drenched the cereal with chocolate milk and imitated how his mum would complain that he'd eaten all the cereal and I laughed. His parents travelled constantly so he and his siblings were mostly alone. Every time I slept over we ran to the ferry because it was a ten-minute walk and we'd leave his bedroom with three minutes to spare. His eyes were like the light blue sky at dusk.

This sugar-coated boy had a shisha in his room, herbs on his balcony and French windows that opened to the ocean. I hardly got a word in but when I did he listened and thought I was hilarious. His music was ethereal but beautiful, like a dream I didn't know I'd had. We played a game one night where we ran around the neighbourhood then ran into the ocean in the early hours of the morning.

I certainly didn't say I was well yet. But I needed the swim. I needed him. I needed to strip off my clothes and dive beneath a black sea. I needed to surface with my eyes wide open and look across at him in a moment of shared bliss. I needed to laugh.

He was a breath of fresh air and I loved him for that.

In the same way I had, he'd chosen the course because it was fitting, it was structure, it was something to satisfy the grandparents, it was acceptable, it was *good* and he liked art so it was appropriate.

But he *loved* music.

He saved enough money for a plane ticket and $1000 for his pocket and then left university to hear the sounds of the world and to seize an opportunity to record in a studio in Berlin.

He moved on. Change is inevitable.

And I remember walking sluggishly out of the gates of Callan Park at uni, about to commence the two-hour walk, bus, walk, bus, walk home, with the sun gripping the collar of my black coat and my bag's leather strap biting into my shoulder. It was just after one and I was *so* jealous of him.

That's when I caught myself thinking, *I can't wait until I finish uni so that I can do nothing but write.*

I stopped and leant against the pale blue wall of a car mechanic's building. I stood there for a while.

When I was fifteen and girls were thinking of their outfits for Friday night, and how they were going to fish for alcohol from strangers outside the liquor store, I was dreaming, *I can't wait until I finish school so that I can do nothing but write.*

I'd spent two years underwater, and my dream had gotten wet. Life had gotten in the way. I'd let my dream disintegrate.

My mind was racing as I leant against that cool wall in the winter sun. What if I finished uni and straightaway got a job (I had to pay the rent somehow), thinking, *I can't wait until I save enough to quit so that I can do nothing but write.* What if a few years slipped through my fingers and I found myself pregnant, thinking, *I can't wait until the kids have moved out of home so that I can do nothing but write.* What if the mortgage is still too heavy after my husband loses his job and so I'm back in the workforce thinking, *I can't wait until I retire so that I can do nothing but write.*

I was so jealous of the sugar-coated boy. I was so jealous of how he could just do it. I was so jealous of how he could step from the path and chase something over the horizon that he couldn't even be sure was there.

Suddenly it dawned on me.

Why couldn't I?

There was no answer. There was no reason.

I too could chase the horizon. There were no rules. My time was now.

It was quite possibly the most terrifying, and yet the most exhilarating idea my mind had ever conceived.

I recently learnt that actor Jim Carrey was homeless at the age of fourteen after his father lost his job. When asked about the experience, he said: 'I learnt that nothing is safe, so you may as well do what you love.'

Nothing is safe. Everything changes.

What if a relapse was to drag me beneath the surface once more, and I was unable to write again with the cold scaly hands of depression tightening around my neck? What if I were to end up a bitter woman having worn the jacket sewn with the dull fabric of mediocre expectations and social normality? And what if I died old in a body that was intact and well maintained because my days had been safe? Nothing to say I'd lived. No scars from dark times, no leathered skin from kissing the sun, no broken heart from loving passionately, no hoarse throat from laughing deeply, no aching legs from walking great miles and no tired eyes from witnessing majestic sights.

Did I dare chase the horizon?

I don't even know if what I seek exists beyond that thin blue line.

•

The first person I spoke to about this realisation was a girl who was the most beautiful in our senior year. She was ranked third in accelerated maths, brought me a teddy bear in hospital that was almost bigger than me and laughed because her boyfriend had given it to her for Valentine's Day. Her laugh is contagious and you could always hear it from the other end of the school. She sits among the five people whose opinion I trust the most.

She is the girl with the chestnut hair.

Shadows swam across the sea as the sun moved in and out from behind the clouds. We hadn't seen each other for quite a while but it never mattered with her, we'd pick up where we'd left off as if no time had stood between us. It's funny because that day we'd walked around the headland, and down through the trees on the wooden boardwalk that leads you out onto the dog park on a concrete path that is the colour of stale bread. I was midway through telling her how much I hated the path I was on and how I felt like time was passing but that I was going nowhere, when I blurted, 'Can we cut through the park? I hate walking on concrete.' She laughed, we stepped onto the grass and the conversation continued.

Ironic really.

When I was in hospital in year 12, my friends were arranging to go travelling together. After graduation, three of my closest friends began working full-time, saving every dollar to hold in their purses when they boarded planes in April, set for the other side of the world.

For those months when I wasn't allowed to be left alone, I watched programs on the satellite station National Geographic Adventure by day and by night, I travelled through dreams.

I was at university when they left, and in the many months that followed, my reinstated Facebook feed was inundated with epic pictures as they walked through *my* dreams. There was one picture of the girl with the chestnut hair on a camel in Morocco and I was beyond jealous. I knew that my dreams would never compare to the way the brilliant orange sand would shift beneath the soles of her feet, or the way her baked, dry clothes would feel on her skin in the afternoon Moroccan sun.

One of the girls came back to study Medical Science, the second came back to study Commerce and Law, and the other came back to study Psychology and Law. I felt that they'd done it the right way and only wished I could have done the same.

'But you've got your whole life to travel,' she told me.

These girls had seen, smelt, heard, tasted and touched more of the world than an episode on the National Geographic channel could ever encapsulate. I was only one year ahead of them at university, and they'd already gone halfway around the world.

I felt I was on a concrete path.

'Then do something else,' my friend said as we walked across the grass. 'Go to an advisor, they can recommend you to other courses, maybe journalism?'

'I want to write novels, they don't have a course for that, and I'm already halfway through, it would be a waste.'

In a year and a half I would graduate, and I would have a piece of paper to attach to my résumé that would say I was capable of committing to something, that I showed initiative, that I was creative, and smart enough to have a degree.

I wasn't going to be an art teacher, I wasn't going to own a gallery and I wasn't going to curate. The silly thing was if I did graduate and finally find the guts to write all the time, I wouldn't actually need the swanky résumé.

'Then defer,' the girl with the chestnut hair said.

'I can't.'

'Why not?'

My words got caught in my throat and I remember a kind of opening of my lungs. The winter air had a clean bite.

I told her a handful of reasons why I couldn't defer and we walked for a while in silence. Blood pulsed in my temples. The hairs on my arms were raised yet it wasn't from the wind. I was terrified because I knew then that my rationale carried little weight. My 'reasons' were tepid water vapour.

Half-hearted excuses.

•

When I was fifteen I memorised a quote from the film, *The Curious Case of Benjamin Button*, written by Eric Roth. It was one of the first quotes to permanently mark my skin.

The protagonist sends a letter to his love. The letter, in my opinion, is a remarkable summation of life and what it means to truly *live*.

It inspired me because it broke down stock-standard ideas on how to best navigate through life and instead presented a reality where I was free to forge my own path. It legitimised my desire to travel the world writing books.

The letter also proposed one poignant life goal that I then aspired to achieve. It was taking pride in the life you are living.

Was *I* proud?

When I was still fifteen, Mum was driving me to school in Manly. On the route, as you drive over the headland from Freshwater Beach to Queenscliff, there is a bend in the road that is quite bold. As you round the corner you leave behind a string of houses, and the right-hand side of the road drops away allowing you your first glimpse of the ocean. I'd been driven to school that way many times before, and many times after, but that morning was one of those moments that have been written in bold on the pages of my past.

I know it was winter because I was wearing compulsory black stockings beneath my school skirt. I hated the stockings, much preferring to feel winter's bite. On my lap was the brown leather folder I'd bought for $1 at a charity store. In it were three non-lined notebooks and countless sheets of paper, every page decorated entirely with words. My first novel lay safe within the folder's thick leather skin.

I was bouncing my knee, as I do when I am excited, nervous, restless and ready. The night before I had read an email from a motivational speaker, Glen Gerreyn, who had visited my school. Words cannot describe his energy, or the intensity with which his body glows. His hope is infectious.

He had published two books when I first met him and I asked him at the end of the seminar, 'How?'

He'd been surprised when I'd said I had almost finished writing a book and he asked me to send him a chapter, which I did the second I got home. The following night he sent me his number and said, 'When you finish your book, call me and we'll talk about publishing.'

I remember reading it in Mum's office. It's a small room with a green feature wall and a ceiling light that doesn't shine as bright as those in the rest of the house, and I jumped up in the lime-green haze and yelled out for my whole family to come in and read it.

I was so excited at the idea of publishing a novel at fifteen that I missed the most important thing he said, 'Wow! You really are a writer, Sophie.'

'Imagine if it gets published, Mum!' I said in the car on the way to school, beaming.

'Yeah, well the exciting thing is if someone picks you up and runs with you now, they're going to look at it and think if this is what you're doing now, imagine what you'll be doing when you're nineteen or twenty, or even what you'll be doing in ten years when you're twenty-five!'

I nodded silently with a wide smile plastered to my face.

A moment later the car rounded the bend and I got my first glimpse of the sea shimmering in the yellow morning light.

Around that time, Mum and I walked into a bookstore in Chatswood. It was the kind that makes your eyes widen at the sight of bookshelves lining every wall, stretching right up to the high ceilings. It was the kind where you climb a moving ladder to reach the top.

'I'm going to have a book on a shelf in here one day.'

'I believe you,' Mum told me. 'But I think you'll have more than one.'

.

Was I proud of being at university, studying Visual Arts, majoring in painting?

A course I liked but did not love. A course where the sluggish commute far outweighed the joys of the lectures, tutorials and time in my studio.

I had started working in a surfboard factory but was I proud to be spraying surfboards and painting with resin? It paid more than any café or bar. My boss cared, and it was a *cool* job. But foam dust got in my ears and the chemicals burnt my nostrils when I wasn't wearing a mask.

Was I proud when I cleaned out my room before moving out of home, and found that brown leather folder, the one I carried every day under my arm for two years, deep in the belly of my wardrobe? Covered in dust, its skin was a pallid grey. Furry pale blue and green spots of mould had bred near the zipper line. Worse still, the zipper now had crusty teeth that were almost impossible to separate. My brown leather folder smelt of damp, forgotten words.

Was I proud?

Only in asking that question did I realise how disappointed the fifteen-year-old girl, striding out of the bookstore with her mum, would have been to see me now. I had failed her.

'I'm considering deferring uni.'

That is how it started, four simple words. My delivery was weak and the words dribbled out of my mouth onto my shirt. But I repeated them, again and again until they solidified on my tongue.

I guess the reason why the people who love you the most are sometimes the least encouraging is because they care. They don't want to see you get hurt.

But I was already hurting.

Writing is my salvation, and it was trapped in a rank folder that had been chewed up and swallowed by my wardrobe.

One feared for me because 'not many people make a living out of writing'.

Not everyone can make *money* out of writing.

But I can make a living, because when I write I am *living*. It doesn't matter how much money I have in my pockets as long as I have a sore hand from putting pen to paper, and a weary mind at the end of the day from dreaming . . . having invented something from nothing.

Another who loved me said he didn't care what I did as long as I was happy. I guess I wanted to hear him say it was the right thing to do, but in hindsight I needed to realise for myself that I was making the right decision.

And then there was Mum, my greatest critic. She is the person whose opinion overrides all others'. But she is also the one who has always maintained a degree is one of the most valuable gems you can pocket.

It is a key that opens doors.

Mum so badly wanted me to open the doors she was never given the chance to. I only hope she knows what a remarkable life she has lived without that piece of paper.

At the same time, I cannot deny the truth in her argument. Education empowers the individual. Intelligence fortifies character and wisdom feeds the soul.

But, in my case, my mum's argument was denying me what I truly wanted. Her argument had me walking on an even concrete path that was grey, repetitive and it hurt my ankles.

Four weeks before semester two started, I told her what I had been considering and she sold the argument I'd heard a hundred times before and she sold it well. I only had a year and a half to go, that's easy! I just needed to get it out of the way and then I would have all the time in the world to write.

For the first time, however, I didn't believe it. By this point I had spent four weeks repeating to myself *I'm considering deferring uni.* My words grew strong, such that when I found myself lying in bed a week before the beginning of the semester, I knew I would be more disappointed in myself for *not* deferring than I would be if I deferred and failed.

A week later I was sweating as I walked through the gates of Callan Park and up Darling Street to the bus stop. I don't know if it was because I'd worn too many layers and it was abnormally humid for winter, or if it was because I had suspended my course and was reassuring myself that I was not an idiot.

When I arrived home, I don't think I'd realised how unnerving my loved ones' voices would be as I told them what I'd done . . . Mum was so disappointed. She's certainly not one of those sporting mums who tries to live out their own dreams in their children but I knew she was mourning the opportunity she'd missed out on. She'd wanted better for me.

For two days, I fought to believe I had made the right decision.

I was *fighting*, because I no longer believed it. I wasn't winning. All the courageous soldiers I had rallied beneath my skin had deserted me, and I wanted so badly for Mum to tell me that I was doing the right thing, but she couldn't. She wouldn't have believed her words. She wouldn't have sold them. She would have been lying.

Show them.

I knew what I wanted, and the only way anyone would back my campaign was if I took charge. I needed to show them. I needed to prove them wrong.

On the Wednesday, I sent Glen Gerreyn an email. I told him who I was (knowing he probably wouldn't remember me – he speaks to 100,000 people a year). I told him that six months after he spoke to me about publishing I'd experienced my first symptoms of bipolar. I told him how I sank, how I drowned, how I made it to the surface and how I was able to breathe once more. How I died and how I lived. I'm not sure quite what possessed me to write the email; maybe deep down I needed someone to say they would rally behind me. I told him how I was working on a book called *China*, and how I wanted it to save at least one person from experiencing the darkness of the abyss like I had. I told him how I wanted to change someone's story for the better.

I had this idea that if he had wanted to help me publish four years ago, maybe he'd want to help me now. I was thinking that it would be easier to write knowing that there was a good chance of someone wanting to read it at the end. I wasn't thinking that he would reply.

Glen called me that afternoon; he told me he had known exactly who I was as soon as he'd started reading my email.

The very next thing he said was, 'Wow! You really are a writer, Sophie . . .'

My smile stretched from ear to ear and I suddenly felt as if I were standing in the lime-green haze of Mum's office.

'I think you've made the right decision with university, you have a voice and it needs to be heard.'

When I had lunch with him and his wife I laughed at how I'd achieved more as a writer in two and a half weeks than I had as a painter in a year and a half. I was writing my book, I was speaking to an agency that invests in young writers, as well as their collaborative press company. I had been accepted into a course run by the Australian Theatre for Young People and we were being taken away for a week to work with three of Australia's best playwrights. In addition, I was about to go to Green Island, on the New South Wales' south coast, to interview a surfing legend for Australia's leading surf magazine. Admittedly, I had practically banged on the door until I was let into the magazine's office, determined for the head editor to realise my potential.

The ruthless knocking was something I would never have been driven to do in the art world; I would never have had the determination to bang down exhibition gallery doors.

At lunch I was so animated because I just couldn't believe how powerful harnessing your passion makes you.

Your passion empowers you, because you will chase that dream over the horizon, you will chase it to the ends of the earth. You will keep banging on doors no matter how many are slammed shut. And you will find the courage to 'run like China' because deep down you realise you will never know happiness in its purest form unless you live out this dream.

When I interviewed Pam Burridge for *Surfing World*, she said, 'If you want it enough, you will get it, because you simply will not stop until you do.' She knew what she was talking about. Her passion had made her one of Australia's first professional female surfers and a world champion.

Sitting at lunch that day, Glen turned to me and I watched his dark eyes melt to smooth caramel as he smiled. The only other eyes I'd ever seen look at me in this way were Mum's. The intensity of his gaze was indescribable. Glen had *so* much faith in me.

With conviction that set my world on fire, he told me, 'Sophie . . . your future is so bright.'

•

Movie director James Cameron famously explained that when you film something and put your name to it, no matter how trivial it may be, you become a director.

At parties it sounded cool that I made surfboards, cool that I studied art. But the reality was, I let two things occupy my time, when my true desire lingered on the distant line between the sky and the sea.

I make surfboards and I'm at uni, but I really want to be a writer.

In that first week after having suspended my course, I was house-sitting, curled up on a dark blue couch with the dog at my feet, my laptop on my knees and the fire roaring. I finished chapter two when suddenly it dawned on me. My name is on it. I *am* a writer.

•

In September 2013, when I was writing *Running Like China*, I saw the man with the snow beard for the last time. The two years I'd spent with him was a fair portion of my life as a teenager; especially as they were the longest, most difficult days I had ever lived.

He watched me drown; he saw me breathe again.

When he had told me that he was retiring in four months, I'd felt a tightness in my chest. For a while I ignored it. Then, in the final few weeks within his care, he needed blood work from me to check my levels. For three weeks I forgot to do it, and I think that, subconsciously, I was hoping that if he didn't get the levels, he'd have unfinished business and wouldn't be able to retire.

In the end the lines in his skin told me that he deserved a rest so I went and had the blood tests done.

Leaving him was bizarre. He'd given me my life back. He is a main character in *my* story, but what am I in his? He saw hundreds of patients over the years and saved many lives.

I was terrified about changing doctors.

I told him all the other doctors I'd met were shit and that I probably wouldn't find another one as good as him.

His cheeks were the colour of pink rose petals as he chuckled. I think he was as flattered as he was amused.

I told him I didn't want to have to tell my story to someone else. I didn't want to start all over again. Then I confessed that I was nervous, and he laughed.

'They say that that's all therapy is . . . two nervous people in a room hoping for something better.'

As I walked out his door for the last time, I told him, 'I'm writing a book and soon I'll send you a copy and you'll be able to see how well you have shaped its chapters.'

Suddenly I could see us for what we truly were, an unlikely, yet beautiful connection between a doctor and his patient – an old wise man and a girl.

.

Once you realise that the ground you're standing on actually *isn't* safe, you'll discover there is no need to fear that step, no matter how 'terrifyingly' bold.

There is no need to fear.

We don't want to risk changing our place in space and time in case we like the new one less and find we can't go back. But nothing is static, we are moving through space and time as it is. You cannot deny change. You cannot control it.

Identifying the very things that set my world on fire as a fifteen year old, and then finding the courage to abandon my prescribed schedule in pursuit of *the impossible*, has allowed me to rediscover the ambitious girl who is as stubborn as hell. I have found the girl who questions *everything* because she knows she will never know all the answers. I have found the girl who writes and dances beneath the silver moon. I have found the girl who will forever chase something greater than herself.

I have found myself.

23

Natural Highs

It's hard to surf in a psychiatric hospital.

For months I was a fish out of water. My skin was dry and scaly and my lips were flaking. I was disoriented, forever wandering until I rediscovered my place in the ocean.

When I lay on my surfboard again in late 2012, after months on dry land, the wax felt foreign on my skin. I was off balance, I couldn't duck-dive as deep and my arms were aching by the time I made it into the line-up.

When I stroked into my first wave and rose to my feet, my heart truly started to ache.

My mind remembered what my body had forgotten. I realised that I was no longer in sync with the ocean, and instead found myself so disheartened that I turned around and paddled straight in.

.

Before I experienced my first episodes in 2011, I was sponsored for boards by a local shaper. When I came home from my third hospital admission in February 2012, he offered me a job spray-painting the surfboards. It was good in that it gave me something to do. More importantly, however, he didn't mind that I had stopped competing and instead he started making me alternative boards. I left my performance boards on the shelf and paddled out on fish and dumpster boards. Both designs are typically shorter and thicker, making them more playful.

My boss made me several different models in a bid to get me excited about the water again but each time I mustered up the courage to paddle out, my legs would be so wobbly I'd soon give in and wash ashore on my stomach. The year passed with only a handful of attempts.

It was not until he told me just to forget about how I *used* to surf and pretend I had never competed that my attitude started to shift. I began thinking about all the little things that had thrilled me when I was nine years old and learning it all for the first time. I remembered how it felt to stand for the first time; how I'd sprinted across the sand to Mum and Gee, telling them over and over what I'd just done. I thought of the first time I did a cutback, rode backhand, jumped off rocks to surf a point break or paddled out to a reef break.

Suddenly, I wasn't grieving those experiences. I was excited knowing I was about to have the pleasure of learning them all over again.

This coffee-coloured, coffee-scented man with shorts as short as the seventies is one of the most generous human beings I have ever known. He is my boss, my friend.

He gave me back my ability to dance on water.

Returning to the surf also gave me strength, both physically and mentally. The sea truly is my greatest teacher, and it has reminded me that the rough waves and calm waters of my moods are not something to fear; they are something to embrace.

In the same way I ride waves, I can ride down the face of depression, sink into its belly, throw my body into the turn, race down the line, lift up to the lip and fly off the back, making it out into a safe open channel victoriously.

If I am held beneath and tossed like a rag doll, I know to remain calm, and to savour the air in my lungs because inevitably I will float to the surface.

If I believe I can control it, it will ruin me.

I can, however, ride it out. *Patience* underpins survival.

And so I paddle out each day, arms digging deep, knowing waves will come at me whether I like it or not. Sometimes I sail smoothly beneath the turbulence and rise to the surface with a stretching smile. Other times I won't duck-dive deep enough and I'm ripped off my board. The ocean tears at my limbs but I know not to fight it. I surrender. I relax; the ocean lets go and I resurface.

When I make it to the line-up, I catch my breath and admire the way the sky rests on the sea.

A wave climbs out of the deep and I turn, paddle, rise to my feet, swoop down the face and fly up towards the lip. The bliss is indescribable.

.

Rediscovering the natural highs I cherished as a child has allowed me to find joy in my life again.

I worked myself up recently, angry and annoyed that I couldn't partake in what everyone else was doing. The boy with blue glaciers melting in his eyes and I were driving with grey rain on the windshield. As we stopped at a red traffic light, he turned to me and said, 'There is a reason you can't. I honestly believe it. They're all drinking and doing drugs and it's fun now but they're screwing up their brains. You need your brain, even if you don't know why yet. You're going to do something important . . . something special with your brain. Trust me, there is a reason.'

Looking back at the year I spent wearing my porcelain mask, I swallowed pills and drew thick clouds of smoke into my lungs, all the while thinking I was happy. But the truth is, nothing compares to a laugh that is honest or a genuine smile, the kind that you cannot control.

Artificial highs are fleeting; they last only for as long as the drug is in your system.

Real ecstasy, on the day when you kiss the sky, meet your soulmate, taste the rain, achieve the impossible, lose yourself, find yourself, laugh so hard you burn a hole in your stomach, watch a full moon rise, touch snow for the first time . . . Moments of *real* ecstasy stay with you.

In a recent journal entry I wrote:

Water turns to milk. The horizon is glazed with pink cream. I rest my palms on the sea at dusk.

Did I forget this?

Did I forget how this felt? Did I forget how delicately my hands lie on the smooth surface? Did I forget how it feels to be enveloped by this dark splendour?

The air is still, and yet, out here, I am breathing something else.

•

For me, remembering my appreciation for natural splendours has helped me to rekindle the flames that once burned so magnificently inside my ambitious fifteen-year-old self. I've rediscovered how it feels to live gloriously within a crowded hour.

Even more importantly, my appreciation for the earth and the sky and the sea has allowed me to see beauty in the place where I tried to end my life.

I grew up on that headland; I was carried onto it as a week-old baby; I stood on it and watched whales breach in a sapphire sea before school when I was seven; I kissed my first boyfriend on it when I was thirteen . . . then it became the place where I attempted to leave this earth.

Walking around the headland now, at almost twenty years of age, the sun slips through the clouds and I watch the grey grass turn green and the grey ocean turn blue. The sea breeze cleanses my palate and I feel proud. I am standing here, alive, and I smile because it's an achievement. I thank the sky for the gift of air in my lungs and enjoy the enormity, depth, power and tenderness of the ocean.

Epilogue

I became China.
Reborn.
That's how I survived.
For over a year, I wore a china porcelain mask.
China stood bright and alive, casting a shadow over the one who was sick.
It gave Sophie time; pink blood scars became soft white petals.
She was safe from prying eyes.

But in the end, I underestimated the fragility of my porcelain skin, and the mask became my face. I refused to take it off, denying the existence of my former self.

Inevitably, I cracked and a thousand China pieces lay scattered across the floor.

•

In the months since my relapse in early 2013, I have laughed harder, cried less, spoken with an air of confidence, painted life on canvases, decorated pages with words, kissed the sun and walked beneath the silver moon.

Bipolar disorder, however, has not gone away. I am simply learning to live with it.

Today I am not without a care, nor am I without a want or grief.

But I *am* running.

I am running like China, naked and unbound.

Note from Sophie

Every story and every battle with a mental illness is different. I hope aspects of my story help others to find their way through their own bad times. Whether it is you or a loved one dealing with depression, anxiety or any other mental illness, my message is, be patient. This storm will pass. And there is help for you, always, so please don't ever think you have to wait it out on your own. There will be setbacks, sometimes big ones, and possible relapses, but there will also be moments that take your breath away for all the right reasons. My message is to hold on, because it's in the silence between lightning and thunder that we not only find each other, but also find hope. It took me a while to learn this and that's okay. Everyone is on their own journey moving at their own pace. Everyone will have their own ways of coping and their own ways of dealing with their illness.

Just before this book was published I was readmitted to hospital for a week. My doctor had been working on adjusting my medication and after a few weeks of that I began rapid cycling and experiencing mild psychosis. A surge of dark waves was dragging me down again. My family knew things weren't right before I did and, as much as I dislike it, I know that going into hospital is all part of dealing with Bipolar and recognising when I need help. This admission was more about fixing the chemical balance and getting the medication right than anything else but dealing with any setback is emotionally difficult. Acknowledging that is important. And for me, at a time like this, getting back to basics by eating well, exercising, meditating, getting enough sleep and having a doctor I trust, becomes really important.

I have been asked several times recently if I have employed any exercises or strategies to cope with episodes of depression and/or mania. I have. One of the key things is 'The Letter'. Though it is applicable for both highs and lows, my letter is intended for me to read by myself when in a suicidal state.

The exercise involves writing a letter to yourself when stable to read when you are unwell in an effort to remind you of the normality of a lucid state. It is designed to ground you, and remind you why you must fight for a healthier self.

The letter is personal and you are free to write whatever you want. Below are some suggestions to get your pen moving if you feel stuck.

You may like to write down:

· How important your family is, why you love them, what you love about them
· Things that make you happy
· Your dreams, hopes and aspirations
· Quotes that inspire you
· What excites you, makes you want to move, makes you want to dance
· Songs that lift you
· What it feels like to be in love, to feel love and to feel joy
· A promise to yourself to endure the long winter of depression.

This is my example:

Dear China,

> *This storm will pass. I know it will because it has before. You've heard black and purple clouds thunder and you've seen the sea turn to mud. But you have also seen the water clear, and dived back into the turquoise drink. You have also seen the sun pierce through the clouds, and watched as the sky turns peach pink.*

*I know you feel like you cannot bear a second more
of this. I know your skin is shrinking . . . I know that it is
choking you. I know that you are devastated at the drop
of a hat. I know your tears are real because you are truly
hurting. I know you want to escape and I know you want
to fly, landing in a pool of nothingness.*

*I know you feel like you cannot bear a second more of
this but you have to.*

*You HAVE to because when the clouds do part, it will
be worth it. I promise you it will be worth it so please, I'm
begging you . . . wait until they do.*

*Your sister is so beautiful, and she deserves her big
sister. She is one of the funniest people you know and you
CANNOT leave her. It will destroy her; her jokes will never
be as colourful because she will never laugh as deeply.*

*Your mum is the strongest person you know, and yet it
will break her. She told you that giving birth to your sister
and you were her greatest achievements. You CANNOT
steal yourself from her. She will spend the rest of her life
wondering what she could have done differently.*

*Your dad will stop laughing at his own jokes; his days
will pass slowly and his heart will ache because he will
miss you in a way that only a father could. He's always
been so proud of you. You're his little girl . . . You CANNOT
abandon him.*

*Writing essays, prose, poetry and plays makes you
happy, even if you don't feel like it does right now. The*

salty sea, the silver splendour in the night sky, inappropriate jokes, salmon steak with dill sauce, oak trees,
painting, running, philosophy, surrealist and conceptual
art, rock pools, far horizons, a boy in your bed, adventures
and street food . . . they all make you happy, even if you
don't feel like they do right now.

You're free when you're facing a wind that screams.
You're free in the indigo ocean soup at midnight. You're free
when laughter rolls across your family's dinner table. You're
free when you love.

A grey downpour makes you want to dance. A wild,
roaring ocean excites you.

You want to move when surrounded by trees. You want
to move in the mountains.

You cannot leave this world, because you are going
to do something incredible with your existence. You are
going to travel to lands unknown and write stories about
unknown people. You are going to have a colourful tapestry
because you are going to walk through orange mountain
villages; you're going to lose yourself in the Sahara and
swim in all seven seas. You're going to stand beneath
hundred-year-old trees, meet people with a different point
of view, drink tea in houses built differently from yours and
walk off the track with bare feet.

'One crowded hour of glorious life is worth an age
without a name.'

This depression will pass, I promise, and when it does, you will live gloriously within one crowded hour.

And when you find those moments of magnificence, you will turn around, look back on where you are right now and you will think, this is why I waited.

Please . . . wait out the storm. It will pass, I promise. It will be worth it, I promise.

Love from China

P.S listen to 'Oh Sailor' by Mr Little Jeans. Close your eyes and imagine the ocean blue.

This book is my letter to you. To show you that, with support, it will pass for you too. Wait it out, it will be worth it!

But please don't be afraid to seek help, or to talk about how you feel. Nobody should have to ride through the storm of mental illness without assistance. Your GP can be a starting point but here are some other contacts to help you make sense of how you feel and to find the information and support that you need.

Helplines

Primary National Emergency Number: 000
Lifeline Australia: 13 11 14
Beyond Blue: 1300 22 4636
Kids Helpline: 1800 55 1800

Resources:

Beyond Blue: http://www.beyondblue.org.au
The Black Dog Institute: http://blackdoginstitute.org.au
Kids Helpline: http://www.kidshelp.com.au
mindhealthconnect: http://www.mindhealthconnect.org.au
Headspace: http://www.headspace.org.au
Lifeline Australia: https://lifeline.org.au

Acknowledgements

Thank you first and foremost to my mum, sister and dad. You brought me back to life.

I would also like to acknowledge the people who grace the pages of this book. I hope my words have done you justice and shown you just how much you mean to me.

Thank you Laura Enever for your foreword, you're an amazing girl! And thank you to all the friends who have rallied behind me during the last five years.

And then there are the people who have helped put *Running like China* on the shelves. Thank you Kathy Mossop for taking me seriously at the very beginning, Julia Stiles for wholeheartedly believing in my work, Rob Pearson for making the first edit possible and Sally Macmillan for your careful eye. Thank you Selwa and Linda Anthony for not only representing me as well as you do, but also loving and supporting me every step of the way. And a big thank you to Brian for delivering my first contract to my door on my 21st birthday!

Finally, I would like to thank everyone at Hachette Australia and Hachette New Zealand. Thank you Vanessa Radnidge. From dancing with me at the Sassy Awards to editing the final pages, thank you for *everything*. Thank you also to Louise Sherwin-Stark, Justin Ractliffe, Fiona Hazard, Chris Kunz, Deonie Fiford, Ashleigh Barton, Jackie Money and everyone else who worked tirelessly on this book in the office and all the sales staff around the country who believed in this book and put their heart into connecting my story with readers.

hachette
AUSTRALIA

If you would like to find out more about Hachette Australia,
our authors, upcoming events and new releases you can visit
our website, Facebook or follow us on Twitter:

hachette.com.au
twitter.com/HachetteAus
facebook.com/HachetteAustralia

If you would like to find out more about Sophie you can visit
her website or follow her on Twitter or Instagram:

Sophiehardcastle.com
twitter.com/Soph_Hardcastle
instagram.com/sophie_hardcastle